William Boyd Carpenter

Thoughts on prayer

William Boyd Carpenter

Thoughts on prayer

ISBN/EAN: 9783337283858

Printed in Europe, USA, Canada, Australia, Japan

Cover: Foto ©Lupo / pixelio.de

More available books at **www.hansebooks.com**

Thoughts on Prayer.

BY THE

REV. W. BOYD CARPENTER, M.A.

" For what are men better than sheep or goats,
That nourish a blind life within the brain,
If, knowing God, they lift not hands of prayer.
Both for themselves and those who call them friend?
For so the whole round earth is every way
Bound by gold chains about the feet of gold."
TENNYSON.

A NEW EDITION.

NEW YORK: E. P. DUTTON & Co.,
Church Publishers,
713, BROADWAY.
1881.

TO THE MEMBERS

OF THE

St. James's Holloway Prayer Union,

THESE

"THOUGHTS ON PRAYER"

ARE DEDICATED

IN LOVE.

CONTENTS.

I.
Necessity of Prayer 9   PAGE

II.
Times Adverse to Prayer . . . 17

III.
Heart-work in Prayer 29

IV.
Reality of Answers to Prayer . . 45

V.
Efficacy of Prayer 57

VI.
UNANSWERED PRAYER 67

VII.
BARRENNESS IN PRAYER 91

VIII.
REGULARITY IN PRAYER . . . 105

IX.
MEDITATIONS AND PRAYERS . . 119

X.
SUGGESTIVE OUTLINES . . . . 14[?]

I.

Necessity of Prayer.

"O when the heart is full—when bitter thoughts
Come crowding up for utterance;
And the poor common words of courtesy
Are such a very mockery—how much
The bursting heart may pour itself in prayer."

O GOD, the strength of all them that put their trust in Thee, mercifully accept our prayers; and because through the weakness of our mortal nature we can do no good thing without Thee, grant us the help of Thy grace, that in keeping of Thy commandments we may please Thee, both in will and deed; through Jesus Christ our Lord. *Amen.*

Necessity of Prayer.

Prayer is natural to men. The knowledge of our own weakness is soon forced upon us; but with this conviction there comes another, the sense of dependence on One great, loving, and wise. Out of these springs the necessity of prayer, which is the language of the frail to the mighty—the confession of need, and the instinct of trust.

Every known religion attests this irresistible impulse to pray. Though under the most degraded forms, or lost sight of in the most splendid ceremonial,—the rudest and most revolting Fetichism to the most gorgeous ritual,—the instinct of prayer is found the inspiring impulse of every kind of religious worship.

Men, indeed, will be found to deny, or to undervalue the evidence of this instinct of prayer; but there are times which wring prayer from prayerless lips; times of danger, when all classes find prayer the most appropriate and natural utterance of their lips, and like the sailors in the story of Jonah, cry every man to his God; times of heart-fear, when the whole spirit sends up from the depths of confusion and darkness an exceeding bitter cry, wherein terror and doubt mingle with the unquenchable instinct of prayer; times when, perhaps, death is approaching, and the dark, unexplored confines of the other world begin to loom vast and vague upon an awakening conscience, and the firm citadel of stoutly maintained unbelief is swept away, and prayer rushes forth in such a despairing shriek as burst from the lips of Thistlewood:—" O God, it there be a God, save my soul, if I have a soul!"

It is not the approach of danger or the feeling of fear only which calls forth prayer.

The irresistible disposition is experienced under the influence of feelings widely different from fear. The contemplation of the universe, and the incomprehensible Being who embraces all things, so wrought upon the mind of Rousseau that, in the restlessness of his transports, he would exclaim, "O great Being! O great Being!" The majesty and splendour of nature, brightening and kindling under the beams of the sun, rising upon the rocky heights of Jura, and circling the sky with flame, filled the soul of Voltaire with such awe that he uncovered his head, and, kneeling, he cried, "I believe—I believe in Thee! O mighty God, I believe!"

If the language of prayer is thus natural to all men, and forced at times from reluctant lips, it is natural with an inexpressible sweetness to hearts accustomed to communion with God. The cultivated instinct becomes a rich enjoyment, and an unutterable relief. The high duty becomes the highest privilege. Among all the exquisite pleasures of God's praying children, there is not one they would not forfeit to retain the joy of heart-converse with their Father. Sweeter than the glad moment when he welcomed Rebekah, was the hour of evening meditation to Isaac. Better than the thrill of triumph which shot through the heart of Moses when he heard the thousands of Israel raise their pæan of victory over the vanquished Egyptians, were the days when he beheld the similitude of the Lord, and communed with Him as a man with his friend (Ex. xxxiii. 11). More heart-rejoicing than the loyal acclamations and rivalling enthusiasm of Judah and Israel (2 Sam. xix.), was the time when David's heart talked with God (Ps. xxvii. 4—8), and gathered a gladness more than the increase of corn and wine and oil could afford (Ps. iv. 7). Dearer to Daniel than the lofty titles of Babylon, the gratitude of the king, and the homage of the profoundest Chaldeans, were the intervals when he could open his window toward Jerusalem, and pour out his heart to God's ever-listening ear.

To such prayer was as natural and necessary as the taking of food. On their knees they found strength and wisdom, the courage and patience for all their toil, the relief of all their burdens, and the happiest moments of their lives. Prayer is necessary to heart-growth, and natural because necessary. As the brisk fresh air brings bloom to the cheeks, and brightness to the eyes, so the atmosphere of prayer exhilarates the spirit, and gladdens the heart. To neglect it is not simply to lose enjoyment, it is to impoverish the soul. Let us be convinced of its necessity, and in its exercise we shall find proof that it is natural and healthful to us; while at times we shall rise into the clearer heights of communion with God, where clouds seldom come, and its rapt enjoyment is unbroken by a doubt, and unsaddened by a care. As a little one lying in undisturbed peace upon its mother's breast, so shall we suck and be satisfied with the breasts of consolation. In prayer we shall find the natural satisfaction of all heart-longings; and in the realization of God with us, the highest natural enjoyment of which the spirit of man is capable; for in His presence is fulness of joy.

There are times when prayer is natural to the most careless; but there are also times when all things tend to deaden the spirit of prayer in the most thoughtful and prayerful of God's children. Such times are times of great and extensive activity, when pleasure is busy, and even enjoyments are full of toil. In the ceaseless industry of business and gaiety, amusement becomes hard work. Hard work brings weariness, and weariness is followed by an indisposition for any exertion of the spirit. Such, too, are times of a wide-spread feeling of uneasiness, when a vague apprehension seems to have seized hold upon the minds of all classes, and a strange sense of insecurity begets an unreasoning and universally felt fear. Such are times of noisy religionism and demonstrative piety, when the minds of men are galvanized into an unnatural activity through the spirit of an unwholesome rivalry; when convictions are degraded into opinions, and toil dwindles into talk, and organised Christian effort is strangled in discussion; when an impracticable tenacity of trifles and a stupendous disregard of principles throws the appearance of vitality over a degenerate and dead pietism. In such times the lulling influences of a strained activity, an undefined terror, and a self-asserting, heart-distracting zealotism steal over the spirits of the most watchful of Christ's servants, and often diminish insensibly their vigilance and earnestness in prayer.

A convergence of such times into one period Christ described, and on the description He founded His warning that men ought *always* to pray. He pictured to His disciples times like the days of Noah and of Lot, when the stream of commercial enterprise and prosperity was full and brimming over when the enjoyments of life were seized upon with eagerness, and pleasure varied by industrious inventiveness, and pursued with unflagging diligence; when there was a great deal of religious talk, much ventilating of new opinions, and a good deal of positiveness and dogmatism abroad, and rival sects and new-formed philosophies all claimed the possession of the Christ,—times when amidst so much hurrying to and fro, and so much loud-tongued religion and angry-voiced controversy, the humble, but tried followers of Christ, bewildered and despairing, would yearn for but a glimpse of the gone-by days, when Christ was among men, but would yearn in vain. In times such as these, the spirit of activity would tend to stifle the spirit of prayer, and the sound of conflict and the alarms of coming danger impede its progress and stagger its perseverance. Our Master, foreseeing these times and these dangers, warns His disciples of the tendency and temptation to relax their continuousness in prayer, and speaks to them the parable to this end, that "*men ought always to pray, and not to faint.*"

II.

Times Adverse to Prayer.

"And if by prayer
Incessant, I could hope to change the will
Of Him who all things can, I would not cease
To weary Him with my assiduous cries."

LET Thy merciful ears, O Lord, be open to the prayers of Thy humble servants; and that they may obtain their petitions make them to ask such things as shall please Thee; through Jesus Christ our Lord. *Amen.*

Times Adverse to Prayer.

The parable in which our Lord seeks to stimulate His followers in the duty of prayer, may at first sight seem so conceived as rather to deter than to encourage. He sketches a woman in circumstances in which it seemed more than hopeless to expect success. She is a widow who is bereft alike of the power to enforce her claims, or of the means to win her cause with a bribe. The man she has to deal with is drawn as unmoved by any of the motives which touch even the worst of our race.

There is a rude sense of right in most men's breasts; and the appeal of outraged helplessness is not often made in vain. But this judge was in his very nature incapable of understanding or feeling the force of such an appeal: he was an unjust judge. Again, even in cases where men have no natural and conscientious sympathy with righteousness, the instinct of retribution frequently arouses a fear of God, which impels them to acts of justice; but in the case of the unjust judge there seemed no avenue for the approach of such a feeling: he feared not God. Nor was he moved by that which, as a last motive, is powerful in the most debased natures, the regard for the opinion of other men. He was of that cold, hardened, and unaccommodating character that he neither feared God nor regarded man. There was not a glimpse of light or softness in such a character as this; where there was neither sympathy, nor the sense of right, nor the apprehensions of just judgment, nor the meaner motive of a desire to stand well with the world; and as these several hard features of this hard character became manifest, all hope for the success of her plea would die out of the widow's heart.

What did our Master intend by thus sketching the judge? Does He mean to represent God in any degree as such? Is not the whole portrait framed on conditions of character the very reverse of our best and noblest conceptions of the Divine Father? Do we not expect to find in Him the highest justice linked with the tenderest readiness to stoop to the cry of the distressed and forsaken? In no sense can this harsh character represent God in His relation to man. But as there must be some point of correspondence between the sketch and the condition of Christ's people, this must be sought not in any actual indifference of God to the cries and prayers of His people, but rather in the state of His people at the particular era Christ has been describing. The unjust judge is not the portrait of what God is, but of what, owing to circumstances of trial, and misrepresentations of unreasonable and wicked men, the suffering, waiting people of Christ will be almost tempted to think Him.

To them, in an era of heartless worldliness, shallow religionism, and noisy dogmatism, it might appear that God was absent from them. The cry would be no new one which complained, "Wherefore art Thou absent from us so long? Thou art a God that hidest Thyself;" till the climax doubt rose like the wild note of the storm-bird hovering on the dreary waste of tossing seas,—"Hath God forgotten to be gracious?" All about them they hear a language which haunts them with hideous dread; the voice of the enemy and the blasphemer are heard whispering, "Is there knowledge in the Most High? He will never regard it;" or deepening into the hoarse utterance of half wish, half fear,—"There is no God!" More, more dogmatically than the voice of the narrowest bigot, Providence is declared to be an unscientific conception, and the notion of prayer completely at variance with the understood and fundamental axioms of a higher philosophy—"All things continue as they are." At length, some bolder in speech than the rest, because feebler in scientific knowledge, take up the words of a taunting proverb against Christ's waiting, praying Church; and cry, "Where is thy God? He will not interfere. He who is the eternal God of unerring wisdom is too wise to err in His pre-arranged plan of law, and, therefore, will not acknowledge mistake by interfering at your request to change His unalterable purpose. Why rend the sky with useless plaints to a God whose cold, unchanging laws work evermore towards the great end He has in view, and will not deviate a hair's breadth for all the swelling murmurs of little-witted men? The true and philosophical conception of God is of one absolute and infinite, and unmoved by earthly passions; incapable of pity, which is a weakness, or of change, which is a folly." And this dreary deity, which is, be it noted, the true portrait of the unjust judge transferred to God the Almighty, the suffering and praying children of God are advised to accept as the pure scientific exposition of the mighty Father of spirits.

Harassed by doubts, wounded and terrified by the oft-reiterated assaults and assertions of her enemies, driven to despair at the seeming unbroken stillness of the unanswering heavens, the Church of Christ is as the lone helpless widow, powerless and poverty-stricken. But she is mighty. Though this hideous portraiture of grim and impassive godhead is thrust upon her, she will have none of it. She will not abandon her plea, or accept the description. With this picture of hard, inexorable justice before her, she will not abandon her plea. If it be so—that she is thus weak and poor, and dealing with one whom no cries for pity, or claims for justice, can arouse, and no aspect of misery touch and soften; then nothing remains for her but the might of her weakness in its unceasing supplications, which will take no denial, nothing remains but to weary him out into compliance.

So neither do Christ's people, wearied and dispirited, abandon their praying. They will not yield. They refuse to accept the portraiture. When the power, or the energy to argue against the suggestions of the enemy has forsaken them, they will still persevere in their cry, "We cannot fail, we must beat in at length; or if we perish in the cold cheerless Godhead you describe, yet better perish so labouring, battling, crying for the light, than be false to the nobler instincts and unquenchable convictions of our higher nature, or silence the sweetest music in the book of God."

Then, when their firm resolve is taken, the mist is taken away. Christ's loving hand removes the soul-freezing portraiture, and brings in the much-loved features. The unjust judge fades from view, and God, our *own* God, is there once more. "Shall not *God*," he says, bringing back the true idea of personal, righteous, loving, and watchful rule, "shall not God avenge His own elect which cry day and night unto Him? I tell you He will avenge them speedily."

The cheerless thought of stern machine-like divinity gives way to the warm bright picture of personal and almighty rule. Fixity and permanence, indeed, is there, but not that of cold necessity, but of providential appointment, based on, and ever observant of, the eternal law of righteousness. This law He stands up to defend, and will avenge every breach of it,—rooting out ungodliness, and answering the cry of His pleading people, who, through myriad doubts and fears, have clung to Him.

The lesson Christ enforces is one—*men ought always to pray.* Let the times be unfavourable, the current of public thought against it, and the scientific conceptions of the day seemingly at variance with the very idea of it,—still let them pray. The answer of prayer will be the reconciliation of all conflicting opinions, and the harmonizing of all difficulties; and even though the prayer be long unheeded, and the tumult of those that trouble us increase ever more and more, yet this itself may be God's way of mercy, closing up every door, and hedging about all avenues, that we may be compelled to go forward to the gate of His love, and knock in the confessed hopelessness of grief, and the strength of utter helplessness, till He opens the gate, and draws us in. Go and take your struggling prayers, like fragrant blossoms, wet with your tears, and plant them at His threshold—

> "That if they can they there may bloom;
> Or dying, there at least may die."

But even dying there they will not be lost—perchance, it is even in thus dying they may find a higher life and truer answer. The prayer which loses its life, like the true-hearted Christian who breathes it, may find it. The precious seed will be met with after many days; no longer a parched and decaying thing, but a bright, and strong, and golden sheaf in the wheat-fields of God's glorious harvest yet to come. "Behold, the husbandman waiteth for the precious fruit of the earth, and hath long patience for it, until he receive the early and latter rain. Be patient therefore, brethren; stablish your hearts: for the coming of the Lord draweth nigh" (James v. 7, 8).

III.

Heart-work in Prayer.

―•◇•―

"Our remedies oft in ourselves do lie,
 Which we ascribe to Heaven: the fated sky
 Gives us free scope; only doth backward pull
 Our slow designs when we ourselves are dull."

O Lord, we beseech Thee mercifully to hear us; and grant that we, to whom Thou hast given an hearty desire to pray, may, by Thy mighty aid, be defended and comforted in all dangers and adversities; through Jesus Christ our Lord. *Amen.*

Heart-work in Prayer.

PRIDE and distrustful over-humbleness are two great adversaries to prayer.

Pride suggests to us that prayer is very easy,—that we have only to ask, and we can do that at any time. Over-humbleness puts away from herself all encouragements, and refuses the consolations from the examples of the men of God, who asked and received. These, the over-humble heart whispers to herself, were heroes of God, favoured with special powers, to which she can never aspire.

These two are adversaries to prayer; and, though inconsistent with one another, are often found both influencing the same breast. St. James touches on both of these. When over-humbleness would plead that the examples of successful and earnest prayer are not for her, the apostle answers, "Elias was a man subject to like passions as we are." When pride would fondly whisper that it is easy to pray, we call to mind that it was with earnest wrestling that the "prophet of fire" won his petitions from the Most High.

The example thus given is a most helpful one; for no man in the Old Testament story seemed to have so completely at command the powers and energies of nature. Opposed by the court, plotted against, living a life of almost complete isolation, and feeling himself the lonely witness for God in an age of degeneracy and idolatry, he seems able with a word of prayer to draw down alike the flames and the showers of Heaven. "There shall not be dew nor rain these years, but according to my word." It sounds simple and easy; but St. James shows us that it was not so. That elevation of noble and unswerving faith was not reached without efforts, aye, agonizing efforts, of prayer:

"He prayed *earnestly* that it might not rain." The highest reaches of faith are not attained without struggling, wrestling prayer.

There is, indeed, no reason, but that which pride, or its pale shadow of over-humbleness, suggests, why we regard a spiritual process like that of prayer, to be easy. Nature about us might have taught us how foolish was this belief. The fields are not reaped without toil; and the golden grain of autumn, while it is the proof of God's goodness, is a witness of the toil of man, which has ploughed, prepared, and sowed. The grandest feats of human courage and ingenuity look simple in completion, but the story of their accomplishment is that of much vicissitude: hope battling with unexpected difficulties — new obstacles calling forth fresh energy, intelligence, and patience —till, at last, out of a chaos of constant care, frequent failures, many disappointments, and much anxious thought and toil, has emerged in grand simplicity a monument of genius which excites the wonder of mankind. And this is true of all the really worthy achievements of men. It is true of the engineer, who tunnels the mountain or spans the flood. It is true of the philosopher, who charms listening nations as he unfolds to them, in simple words, the discovery of some hidden principle, which, after long patience, and oft-renewed and often wearied thought, he has wooed and won from coyly ambushed nature. It is true of the man of letters, and even of the man of song, their undying, soul-rousing words are kindled on no easy-smoking altar, but are beaten forth into brightness amid flames hard to keep aglow.

And it is not otherwise of things spiritual. It is very easy indeed to say words on our knees; but it is not easy to pray—to reach that spirit of realized want, intense faith, and vehement desire out of which true prayer springs forth—this is not to be attained by simply falling into an attitude of reverence, and languidly repeating perhaps routine expressions which have lost their meaning. All the witness of Scripture harmonizes with the testimony of facts in nature, that it is not an easy task to pray aright.

"We know not what we should pray for as we ought," is the language of St. Paul; and so far short did the apostles feel themselves of the true spirit of prayer, that they prayed to be taught to pray: "Lord, *teach* us to pray."

And in the prayers often used in public worship, we confess the same. We acknowledge our ignorance in asking; we speak of the difficulties which beset us in praying, and of the things which from our unworthiness we dare not, and from our blindness we cannot ask, and we bewail the listlessness of our hearts, when we plead with Him who is more ready to hear than we to pray. These difficulties, which all those who have prayed the most have felt the keenest, make real prayer hard work, and serve to call our attention to the strenuous efforts which God's praying servants have ever put forth in their supplications. Jacob became a prince in prayer only after wrestling. Seven times the servant of Elijah went to the summit of Carmel to watch for the cloudy answer to prayer, while his master remained with his face between his knees. These were not prayers which cost nothing.

But it may seem strange that there should be so much difficulty; and it may be well to consider the source of it. It does not arise from God Himself; for all His words are full of assurances that He hears prayer, that His ear is not dull, as though it needed much effort to reach Him, or gain His attention. Nor is the cause to be sought in any difficulty in the thing itself; for nothing can be more clear than this, that prayer is but the speaking to God. The promise is simple: "Ask, and ye shall have," (Matt. vii. 7); and the reproach of His love is equally simple (James iv. 2): "Ye have not, because ye ask not."

The cause, then, why prayer is hard work to man must be sought in ourselves, in whom certain conditions must be fulfilled not before God will hear, but simply before it is possible for us really to pray. We can understand how it is that there should be some conditions of prayer. In physical things there are conditions which must be satisfied before an experiment, suppose, can be successfully made. The difficulty does not lie in the mere *doing;* but in securing the proper conditions in which the doing is possible. The difficulty of Archimedes was not in moving the world; but in securing that which was necessary before he could do it, viz., the place on which to stand.

The difficulty of prayer, then, does not lie in the thing itself; but in our failure to fulfil the conditions in which prayer is possible. We are not left ignorant of these. The Bible tells us of four :—

(1.) *Faith.* "Whatsoever ye shall ask in prayer, believing, ye shall receive." But often and often the state in which our hearts are when we pray is not that of living true faith, but rather of a languid acquiescence in the petitions we are presenting.

(2.) *In the name of Christ.* " Whatsoever ye shall ask in My name," says our Lord. And this condition is not fulfilled by simply appending, as a rhetorical or theological ornament to our prayers, the oft-repeated phrase, "through Jesus Christ our Lord;" but rather in the realization for ourselves of all that that expression means, in the deep conviction of Jesus Christ Himself as the power of that prayer,—in the experience that the prayer takes its complexion from the very consciousness of His presence with us, and at His Father's right hand.

(3.) *With the spirit and with the understanding* (1 Cor. xiv. 15). Prayer must not consist of vague platitudes or cold petitions. The utterance of a few accustomed phrases is far different from the definite sense of need, and the strong desire for help, which is to be found in real prayer. A clear head and a warm heart are much needed in life, and not the less in prayer. For though there may be, and doubtless are, times when our sense of need is experienced in a confused feeling of weariness and desolation, yet it is ever well that we should strive clearly to realize what are the wants which bring us to our knees; for warmth of desire is often lacking because we scarcely know our needs.

But neither must we suppose that this knowlege of our wants is identical with the power of clearly expressing them. The need, and the thoughts of the heart, often lie too deep for words. "Light cares speak," said Seneca; "great ones are dumb!" And they are not unreal, but most real prayers which come as one great sob of mute appeal to the God who can help. Better this silent earnestness than the familiar garrulousness of shallow fools. "When thou prayest," said Bunyan, "rather let thy heart be without words, than thy words without heart."

Should these unspoken prayers be a trial to us, let us remember the Spirit helpeth, and maketh intercession for us with groanings which cannot be uttered (Rom. viii. 26).

(4.) *According to His will.* Prayer is not for the gratification of our own wishes, but for the benefit of our spirits; and can only then be true prayer when it is animated by a spirit of submission to His will, whom we believe to be unerringly wise and unfailingly loving. Want of resignation is want of faith. The impatient eagerness of some prayers is ill-concealed pride. True faith is humble, because trustful, and can endure to see her wishes crossed, for she knows that all things work together for good.

These are four conditions of prayer; and we propose to draw from them the idea of true prayer.

A common notion makes prayer little more than an endeavour to get God to take our view of some matter,—that we ask *for* this or *for* that, without regulating our wishes, curtailing their extravagances, or in any way preparing our hearts beforehand for prayer. But this is, we think, a mistake. He who would truly pray must not kneel, impelled simply by his own heated wishes; but under the influence of some high thoughts respecting Him to whom he prays. His first act in prayer will not be passionately to put forward his own wish or will; but to remember that in all things God's purpose of love is unfolding itself among men. His prayer will be an effort—a spirit of striving to pray "according to His will." It is not the effort to make the Creator's purpose bend to our wish and will; but the effort to move our will and wish into harmony with His. It is not the wild pleading of some blind devotee before an uncertain and capricious deity who may perchance interfere in our behalf. It is rather the effort of a humble and self-distrustful though perplexed spirit, striving to rise out of self, and rely upon the Divine love and wisdom, more tender and true than all the puerile hopes and morbid loves of the frail heart which prays.

All this implies preparation of heart for the work of prayer. We are not left alone. His Holy Spirit is promised. He raises within us the sense and realization of the fatherliness of that love to which we appeal. He aids us in the understanding of our own needs, and elevates our spirits into harmony with God's better purposes, and softens them into submission to His will. There is an assurance of success in prayer gathered from the remembrance of this promise: "Thou preparest their heart; and Thine ear inclineth thereto."

Yet much is left to us. Personal effort, regularity, and method are valuable helps to praying hearts. There is a bad habit which much hinders our prayers—the habit of rushing hurriedly from business, or conversation, or amusement to prayer, without thought or preparation. It is bad for the mind to hasten thus, without a brief interval, from one subject to another: it produces an irritation of the brain, just as frequent interruptions do, and leads to feebleness and unsteadiness in the action of thought. It is no less bad for the religious affections. It clouds the spirit of prayer with the hardly-forgotten forms of other things.

We shall not find ourselves falling into this fault, if we strive to realize the necessity of *heart-work* in prayer. If we remember that the whole heart must be transfused with the spirit of Christ-taught love, trust, and submission, we shall endeavour to secure a few moments for silent thought before we pray. We shall strive to collect our energies, realize our needs, and rouse our hearts, when we bear in mind the difficulties which lie on the threshold of prayer, and the obstacles which must be overcome before we can pray.

There is a mutual action and reaction going on between work and prayer. The difficulties, which we ignore in our own hearts, meet us in our work. Want of meeting and vanquishing the threshold hindrances of prayer is a cause why work is often so weary and profitless to us. This is especially true of what is called Christian work. Sunday-school teachers, visitors, and ministers often feel their toil unremunerative—a painful, irksome task, rather than a labour made light with the love of Christ. Perhaps this is the reflection of a neglect of heart-work in prayer. Work is hard to those who make light work of their prayers; but work comes easy to those who have worked hard in prayer.

IV.

Reality of Answers to Prayer.

"How deeply rooted must unbelief be in our hearts, when we are surprised to find our prayers answered! Instead of feeling sure that they will be so, if they are only offered up in faith, and are in accord with the will of God."

Guesses at Truth.

ALMIGHTY and everlasting God, who art always more ready to hear than we to pray, and art wont to give more than either we desire, or deserve; Pour down upon us the abundance of Thy mercy; forgiving us those things whereof our conscience is afraid, and giving us those good things which we are not worthy to ask, but through the merits and mediation of Jesus Christ, Thy Son, our Lord. *Amen.*

Answers to Prayer.

Ill-considered petitions are not prayers. They are idle wishes, which disturb the heart with fancies, instead of elevating it into faith. True prayer needs thoughtfulness and a fit frame of mind; and when trust and self-surrender springing from meditation and uniting with fervent, Christ-born desire, bring us to our knees, prayer becomes an untold delight, soothing our sorrows, tranquillizing our spirits, and hallowing our thoughts. "Prayer," says a modern writer, "when engaged in, in spirit and in truth, free from pride and the troublings of the passions, contains within itself its own answer, in the heavenly calm and repose which it communicates. Like every other good act, it is its own reward. When thus spread out before God, heaven itself seems to descend upon the soul, as we have seen the sky reflected on the bosom of a tranquil lake spread out beneath it."

This is an aspect of prayer which should never be forgotten; but there is a danger in dwelling exclusively on one side of a question; for man's mind is like the common balance, which needs to be double-weighted to preserve its equilibrium. And there is danger lest, in considering the reflex heart-blessings of prayer, we should overlook its real efficacy, and begin to believe that its only value was to be found in its calming effects on our own spirits.

There is a danger lest such a view should lead us to relax our vigilance, and fall victims to the ready delusions of our own hearts. Every one who knows human nature is aware how readily an idle and complacent temperament deludes itself with false assurances that all is well; and most men are self-complacent in matters of religion. Were, then, the subjective peace stealing over the spirit the only answer to prayer, many would falsely conclude that their prayers were answered, by mistaking the unworthy quiet of self-satisfaction for the spirit of resignation and assurance of faith. An easy, unreflecting, and listless religionism would be adopted, instead of the watchful, Bible-studying, waiting faith of God's children; and every advance would be a step blindly made into ever-deepening gloom. The cry of peace, inward peace, would still be heard, but unattested by the witnessing voice of Spirit, Word, and Providence. Sins would grow up unnoticed, rank, and rapid; for, if all sloth leads to sin, sloth satisfied with the name and appearance of religiousness is followed by the worst of sins.

"The first, that all the rest did guyde,
Was sluggish idleness the nourse of sin;
Upon a slothful asse he chose to ryde,
Arrayed in habit blacke, and amis thin;
Like to a Holy Monck, the service to begin.

> " And in his hand his portesse still he bare,
> That much was worne, but therein little redd ;
> For of devotion he had little care,
> Still drowned in sleepe, and most of his daies dedd.
> Scarse could he once uphold his heavie hedd,
> To looken whether it were night or day ;
> May seeme the wayne was very evill ledd,
> When such an one had guiding of the way,
> That knew not whether right he went, or else astray.
>
> *Faerie Queene*, Bk. i. c. iv. 18, 19.

Nor is this sinful indolence and sad self-delusion the only danger which arises from looking for the results of prayer solely within ourselves. There is still another fear lest such an one-sided view should undermine the reality of our religious belief. We can readily see how this may be; for let us suppose that the only efficacy of prayer is the tranquillizing effect of the act of prayer upon our own spirits; then it would appear that the true process which had taken place was not this, that we had asked for a special gift, which we received in answer; but only that we had worked ourselves into a passively happy frame of mind. The idea of a God, to whom to pray, is not at all a necessary part of such a process. It may be sentimentally necessary. It is not logically so.

Such prayer is clearly the outflow of emotions, which, when got rid of, leave a sense of satisfaction behind—a quieting of the mind—not from the fact that anything has been granted, but that an instinct of nature has been obeyed. You are satisfied, just as you are when the swelling strength of sorrow has found its vent in tears. The relief in the pouring forth of prayer, and the shedding of tears, would be analogous. Each would indicate rather the getting rid of something, than the gaining of it ; rather the satisfaction of an instinct than the benediction of the God who made us. And the answer we heard, if it were any, was only the echo of our own prayers reverberating against the walls of our prison-house ; and, if read aright, should be interpreted as the knell of our fond delusions, not the voice of our loving Father, calling to us across the spheres.

Such a representation of the real end and meaning of prayer repels and disgusts us. We feel that it is not and cannot be any fair representation of it, but rather a caricature in the garb of a vain and feeble philosophy. Our notion of prayer in its origin would not have sprung from such a source as this. Prayer, in its simplest sense, did mean asking from God something which we needed. It was the cry of the weak and helpless to the strong. It was the voice of sorrow to Him who could comfort. The language of repentance to Him who would forgive. The cry of the lost to Him who could save. But this mere effigy of it — were it true — would be an argument for abolishing the very word prayer out of every tongue, and substituting for it the subjective satisfaction experienced after giving way to discontent.

Such reasoning would make all things about us unreal, by assuring us that they were only imaged forth by ourselves, not actually existing without us. That rainbow that you speak of, is no real arching bow of beauty, nor any real effect of light and rain-dew. Of that fact you know nothing. This is a conception of it in your mind. You see an image—you may reason about that—but not about the rainbow as such. Since of that you have no real knowledge; only about the image you perceive and see, not about the bow which, in truth, you never see.

What to us are such refinements? The bright bow is there. Its glorious hues of gold and purple, jet and flame, glow and quiver before us. It spans in triumph the dark clouds which are moving in dense swift retreating columns. The emblem of hope —the teacher of purity—the band of charity —the earnest of promise—it rides victorious over the storm. No mere artifice of words, no deadly logic, or captious and captivating argument can rob us of that which we have seen, which our eyes have looked upon.

We who have seen it, know that God gave us not senses to mock, but to guide us. We who have felt, know that God gave us the desire of prayer not to thwart, disappoint, and deceive us, but to comfort, sustain, and bless us. We who deal day by day with things too real to be ignored, too painful to be forgotten, know that what we see and touch and feel *is*, so far as anything is at all. We who day by day kneel and pray, plead His word, cling to His promise, hear His voice, we also know that He *is*, and that He is "the Rewarder of them that diligently seek Him."

And our Bibles confirm our expectations. The prayers it records are not to be measured in value by the peace and tranquillity which flowed through the hearts of those who prayed; but in real answers seen in sensible results. The torrents which swept over the altars on Carmel, and threatened to stay the royal chariot's course, were no mere subjective conceptions in the prophet's or the monarch's mind. The widow of Zarephath, and the Shunammite, saw and clasped in their arms their sons given back from the grave in answer to prayer. The lengthening of Hezekiah's life, and the victory of Jehoshaphat, were real and intelligible blessings which followed prayer. Everywhere the primary idea that prayer is the asking for something which we hope to obtain is, to say the least, pointedly maintained in all Scripture representations; and though the notion of the spiritual elevation which is wrought in the soul by praying is neither denied nor forgotten, yet nowhere is it put forward as a substitute—

> ... "To palter with us in a double sense:
> To keep the word of promise to our ear,
> And break it to our hope."

While, therefore, it is well that we should ever look within our own spirits for the highest, because truly spiritual answers to prayer; let us never forget to bring our prayers to bear upon the affairs of our daily life, upon the practical trials, difficulties, and business around us. Since in victory over this world's toils, troubles, and anxieties faith gains strength and the spirit of prayer fresh confidence.

" Lord, teach us how to pray aright,
   With reverence and with fear;
Though dust and ashes in Thy sight,
   We may, we must draw near.

" We perish if we cease from prayer:
   O grant us power to pray;
And when to meet Thee we prepare,
   Lord, meet us by the way."

V.

Efficacy of Prayer.

"Prayer makes the darkened cloud withdraw,
Prayer climbs the ladder Jacob saw."

ALMIGHTY and everlasting God, who dost govern all things in heaven and earth; Mercifully hear the supplications of Thy people, and grant us Thy peace all the days of our life; through Jesus Christ our Lord. *Amen.*

Efficacy of Prayer.

THE idea that mere inward experiences are the sum total of answers to be expected to prayer we may dismiss as a view which is one-sided; and which insisted on, to the exclusion of any other, fosters spiritual idleness, weakens the firmness of faith, and ignores the broad and comprehensive representations of the sacred Books. We turn to some thoughts which may tend to assure us of the real efficacy of prayer. Our faith in God's promises is feeble, and it is well to rehearse in its ears the noble acts of the Lord.

Prayer is really effectual. True, there are many things which hinder its success, because they rob it of its vital breath. Sin vitiates it. The hands which are held up, defiled with blood, bring down the stern word—"I will not hear" (Isa. i. 15); but the dutiful and obedient child enters at once into the audience-chamber, and never comes empty-handed away. "Whatsoever we ask, we receive of Him, because we keep His commandments, and do those things which are pleasing in His sight" (1 John iii. 22). Unbelief will destroy its energy; but the wrestling, working prayer of the believing man availeth much; and the examples of success are bright and glowing, and strong to dash away the clustering clouds of our unworthy doubts.

We have no lack of witnesses to the real efficacy of prayer. The histories of every age and every people teem with facts too many, too frequent, too clearly consequential to be pushed aside as isolated accidents or strange coincidences. A catalogue of precedents might be compiled so vast in magnitude, so exquisite and varied in detail, so marvellous in results as to challenge the admiration even if it did not win the homage of the most reluctant and doubting mind. The Old Testament and the New—histories ancient and modern—are gemmed with sparkling examples and soul-comforting assurances. We can but lightly touch upon a few.

Does Abraham pray that Ishmael might live before God? The invincible Bedouins of the desert to-day attest the efficacy of his prayer. Does his servant pray at the well in the strange country? The fair bride he brought home to Isaac, shows that he asked not in vain. Does Jacob pray? The softened heart and disarmed revenge of Esau, witness to an answered prayer. Does Moses pray? The ebb and flow of the battle in the plain below, and the gradual dispersion of Amalek, proved prayer not to be valueless. Does Hannah pray? The youthful prophet of Shiloh shows that she has not prayed in vain. Does Samson pray? The waters bubbling up in the moist dry bone, and the bowing walls of Dagon's temple prove that

God hears and answers prayer. Does Gideon pray? The fleece wet and the ground dry, the ground wet and the fleece dry, were more than natural phenomena. Does David pray? Goliath falls, Saul's hostility is baffled, and the peace of Judah is secured. Does Elijah pray? The blackening heavens and the down-streaming rain, cooling and enriching the three years' thirsty land, are God's voice in reply. Does Hezekiah pray? The fallen hosts of Assyria, and the hasty, ignominious flight of the haughty king, prove the power of his prayer. And what more shall we say of Ezra and of Nehemiah, and of Daniel also, of Ezekiel and Jeremiah, and of Manasseh?

And the record of later times is not less fertile. We cannot think of the witness of the church at Smyrna without almost hearing the long, earnest supplications of Polycarp. We cannot bring to mind the unquenchable zeal, heroic courage, and self-denying ardour of Origen, and forget the prayers of his father Leonidas? Who can recall the pious eloquence, vast erudition, and untiring faithfulness of the great Augustine, and be unmindful of the tears and toilful intercessions of his once almost broken-hearted mother Monica? Can truth-loving, freedom-loving men of to-day read the story of England's perils and preservations without a tender recollection of the old man who looked "goodly in his shroud," and of the prayer he prayed amid flame and death? Who that reads Cecil's "Remains" can fail to recall the mother whose tears and prayerful expostulations roused the wrath while they wakened the conscience of her son?

Nor is our own time without its bright evidences. In those days of terrible suspense, when the hearts of English people yearned to leap across leagues of sea and land, and stand beside their endangered brethren in India; the hands that could not help were folded in prayer; and from myriads of Christian churches the oft-repeated prayer went up concerning the rebels: "Abate their pride, assuage their malice, and confound their devices." Through the mutinous district, under the sultry Indian sun, at that time, two English ladies, alone and unprotected, were driving to a place of shelter and safety. One of them carried her newborn baby in her arms. In terror they shrank at the sight of every dusky figure upon the road; for it was only hoping against hope that they would pass unmolested among that territory of foes; and the last glimpse of hope died out of their hearts as suddenly a band of Sepoys rushed upon them and surrounded the carriage. But at that instant, as armed hands of violent men were stretched forth to slay, the unconscious babe at its mother's breast turned in its sleep and smiled; the murderers' hearts failed, the violent hands wavered and dropped, and the carriage with its precious burden passed unharmed. Thousands of miles away loving, agonizing hearts had prayed—" Assuage their malice."

Though these witnessing facts to the real

efficacy of prayer are heart-helping, there is yet a better assurance—that gained from our own experience, for this belongs to a region which we can neither gainsay nor resist. And is there *no* difficulty in our past lives which we have overcome in prayer? No cloud which, even while you knelt, has cleared away? These experiences afford an abiding answer to every cavil, and a ready reply to every ingenious sophistry.

> "A warmth within your heart will melt
> The freezing reason's colder part;
> And, like a man in wrath, the heart
> Will boldly answer, I have felt."

But if you have not felt this? If you can recall no cloud which has melted before prayer, no temptation which you have vanquished upon your knees, no assurance within your own experience that prayer is not in vain, then your need of prayer is all the greater. Then go and pray. Pray, for God bids you. Pray, for He invites you. Pray, for you stand in sore need of help. Pray, that you may prove the truth of the energy and efficacy of prayer. You have abundant encouragements. The promises are clear, great, and precious: " Ask, and it shall be given to you." You may come boldly to the throne of grace for help in every time of need. "He will be very gracious to thee at the voice of thy cry. When He shall hear it, He will answer thee."

> "Were half the breath oft vainly spent,
> To heaven in supplication sent,—
> Our cheerful song would oftener be,
> Hear what the Lord has done for me!"

VI.

Unanswered Prayer.

"We, ignorant of ourselves,
Beg often our own harms, which the wise powers
Deny us for our good; so we find profit
By losing of our prayers."
SHAKESPEARE.

O GOD, whose never-failing providence ordereth all things both in heaven and earth; We humbly beseech Thee to put away from us all hurtful things, and to give us those things which be profitable for us; through Jesus Christ our Lord. *Amen.*

Unanswered Prayer.

"Good prayers never come weeping home." The good man who wrote these words might well feel confidence in doing so, when he recalled the many and abundant encouragements to prayer. The promises of God are boundless in extent, and given with the unfailing guarantee of His covenant in Christ:—" Whatsoever ye shall ask in My name." " This is the confidence that if we ask anything according to His will, He heareth us. Hitherto ye have asked nothing in My name; ask and receive, that your joy may be full." " He that spared not His own Son, but delivered Him up for us all, how shall He not with Him also freely give us all things?" With exceeding great and precious promises, and with such rich proofs of His love, anything like doubt sounds like a dishonour done to Him. But prayers, even good prayers, may yet come unanswered, though perhaps not weeping, home; for there is such a thing as *unanswered prayer*.

The petitions (I will not call them prayers) of openly godless men are unanswered. When the hands are defiled with blood, when the heart regards iniquity, God will not hear. There is a mercy in such denials. The awakening of a spirit of inquiry may result from the experience of unanswered prayer; just as an untoward accident has sometimes been the means of leading to a great discovery or beneficent invention. The interruption in the expected order and working of an engine, arresting attention, leads to the ingenious contrivance which simplifies and gives smoothness to its action.

So unanswered prayer, the interruption of at least the expectation which the promises of God seem to warrant, serves to call our attention to some defect, or drawback—perhaps some fatal self-delusion—which we have cherished in our hearts. It is a wise, even if a bitter discipline; for there may be even deeper knowledge, more heart-searching experience gained in the denial than in the answer of prayer. Let us look to some cautions, causes, and consolations connected with unanswered prayer.

I. *Cautions respecting unanswered prayer.*

The sense that our prayers have not been answered is always fraught with bitter trial, and I doubt not much heart-searching, to God's children. In the first paroxysms of any sorrow, we are inclined to draw very hasty and rash conclusions. "I am cast out of the sight of Thine eyes," we are tempted to cry; or we take up the argument of the blind man, and turn its keen edge against ourselves: "We know that God heareth not sinners; but if any man be a worshipper of God and doeth His will, him He heareth;" and we go away with spirit wounded, and our heart within us desolate, and cry, "God has cast us off, and left us to become like them that go down into the pit."

But this is distrusting God. This is making His wisdom in refusing an argument against His love. It is fretting against the cross; for the unanswered prayer may be a trial to which He calls us, that we may learn to be silent before Him; but we have no right to conclude that He has forsaken us, as long as there is any other possible explanation open. There is, indeed, the case of Saul, whom at the last God refused to answer; but the case is a warning to those who persistently reject God's call to them, and not a discouragement to those to whom the apparent silence of God is a bitter, bitter trial.

Again, a caution is needed against too hastily concluding that our prayers are unanswered. They may have been answered, and through want of vigilance and circumspection, we may have missed the answer.

Prayer is like the lowering of the pitcher into the deep, fathomless well of God's grace. We are careful in letting down the pitcher; but let us remember that to gain the returning blessing we need cautious watchfulness and careful circumspection as we bring up again the brimming vessel. And perhaps we have never thought of drawing it over to the mouth of the well; and there may now be lying the overrunning blessings of answered prayers, waiting for the putting forth of our hands to take.

But while we must thus be careful not to dishonour God by doubt, and never hastily to conclude that our prayers are unanswered, we must also endeavour to keep in mind that there are

II. *Causes and reasons for unanswered prayer.*

One word will express all these causes—inconsistency; for our prayers seem to be left unanswered either because of inconsistency in us, inconsistency with themselves, inconsistency with a greater good.

(1.) *Inconsistency in us.* Prayer cannot be cold, if it is prayer at all. We go to ask for some great good from the loving heart of God, but we go with cold hearts, listless, manner, wandering thoughts, feeble and indolent emotions. Such prayers, it has been said, invite denials. For prayer to win its way to the heart of God it must come from our heart, it must move on the tide of deep real desire. We must *feel* what we say.

> "Lord, when we bend before Thy throne,
> And our confessions pour,
> Teach us to feel the sins we own,
> And hate what we deplore."

To feel the deep necessities of our nature will rouse the strong tide of true earnestness, without which many prayers lie hopelessly stranded in our barren, unmoved hearts. When the vessel is to be floated from the dock, the sluice gates must first be unlocked; and when she has risen on the upbearing waters to the level of the great waters outside, then the locks may be thrown open to let her through. So, too, must real, earnest, deep, passionate desire—the wave of holy vehemence—raise our hearts from the dull, stony level of earthliness to the true height of prayer. For such the gates of Paradise unfold, and the answers of God are clear and many. "The kingdom of heaven suffereth violence, and the violent take it by force."

The *absence of deep real desire*, then, is one cause of unanswered prayer. It is a cause God has promised to remove. "For the Spirit likewise helpeth our infirmities, and maketh intercession for us" (Rom. viii. 26), and in us, with all the strong princely violence which takes no denial, "with groanings which cannot be uttered."

But there is an earnestness in prayer which must never be mistaken for this true holy earnestness we speak of. There is an earnestness which marks, if possible, greater inconsistency in our prayers than cold listlessness. It is the earnestness of a worldly spirit. Prayer to many is only an opportunity of indulging their earthly wishes, the excursion of grovelling fancies. When St. James spoke of the unanswered prayers of Christians in his day, he said, "Ye have not, because ye ask not." No doubt they offered prayer, but not in simple faith and heart-felt earnestness. Nor was this the only reason for unanswered prayer. He spoke of another. He spoke of prayers not lacking in earnestness, but lacking in holiness,— prayers which looked for the gratification of their wishes, their pleasures, their lusts: "Ye ask, and receive not, because ye ask amiss, that ye may spend it upon your lusts." The presence of a worldly spirit is like a weight of lead upon the wings of faith. Anger praying against its enemies; pride praying for its own satisfaction; envy praying against its more successful rivals; tumultuous wrath praying ragingly, blindly, and confusedly; ambition praying for success in life, which never asked for grace; fawning sycophancy praying prosperity in courtly address. These may pray, as they have prayed, earnestly; but such prayers are not "the lifting up of holy hands, without wrath and doubting." Such are regarding iniquity in their heart, and are best blest when the Lord will not hear them.

Well may we, knowing the deceitfulness of sin, examine our hearts ere we pray; and, in every supplication, beseech Him who is all wisdom and love to teach us how to pray.

We may stultify our prayers by a secret protest within our hearts against the granting of our prayers. We pray for some blessing, which in our heart of hearts we trust God will not give us; for we know that it would cause us enforced self-denial. There is a difference to be noted between such prayers and the prayer which springs from an earnest longing to be near and nearer Christ, and asks, heroically asks, with bleeding heart, the removal of every hindrance.

> "The dearest idol I have known,
> Whate'er that idol be,
> Help me to tear it from Thy throne,
> And worship only Thee."

But the prayers we now speak of are those which spring from an insincere heart, which does not mean all it asks. Such are the prayers of those who wish to live to themselves in this world, and with Christ in the world to come. And sometimes this spirit of insincerity will creep in and mar the prayers, and hinder the answers to the prayers, of God's best and brightest children. The desire of some worldly good is too strong for them, and practically they say, "Not Thy will, but mine be done." Oh for our Master's spirit, the complete renunciation of every secret reluctance, the total abandoning of our own wish, our own pleasures or gain, the willingness to suffer as well as the readiness to serve.

The wish for nearness to Christ will overcome the wish for worldly ease, and the heart will cry—

> "I cannot keep me close,—
> Life's stormy sea
> Drives me away
> Far off from Thee.
> I will not murmur
> Whatsoe'er it be,
> So that the cord be strong
> Which binds me near to Thee."

These causes of unanswered prayer, which we have hitherto been considering, have had more or less of sin in them, for they are causes which spring from inconsistency with ourselves. There are other causes, and among them there is an inconsistency which arises more from our ignorance than our fault, but which must be taken into account as a reason for unanswered prayer.

(2.) *Inconsistency with itself.* A child, who has no knowledge of the general laws which govern his own life, may ask his father for two things which are mutually inconsistent, and could not both be granted.

Success in many pursuits depends upon a dark and cloudy day. He will not wish for sunshine who desires good fishing. A victorious war and a prosperous peace cannot be carried on together. Thus we believe it is with the sphere of our prayers. There are things which we may ask for, which in the very nature of the case cannot all be granted, at any rate at the same time. We are unable, doubtless, to understand, as children, how our prayers may sometimes contradict one another; but all the experience of things about us shows us at least that it may be so. Indeed the granting of one prayer may be as a blight upon another. Thus St. Paul's most earnest prayer was for holiness—that he might be like Christ—that he might apprehend that for which also he was apprehended of Christ Jesus. Who can doubt that this was far more his desire than any worldly blessing or bodily comfort? And his experience is that he must bear a constant and painful infirmity that his prayers for higher sanctification may be answered. Caught up in rapt ecstacy into the third heaven, he enjoyed a glimpse of celestial communion; but this rich experience is followed by the painful trial of the thorn in the flesh, probably some bodily infirmity. Thrice he pleads for its removal, but he is denied his request. That prayer was unanswered, because the thorn in the flesh was permitted lest he should be lifted up above measure. It was the cross he needed, that his earnest prayers for holiness and likeness to Christ might be richly answered.

It is a sweet thought that we can rest the choice of answer between our often conflicting and inconsistent prayers with Him, who is too wise to err, too good to cause us needless pain. But the fact of this inconsistency brings with it a most terrible reflection and warning against the want of a spirit of moderation and resignation in prayer. For we may be most vehemently pleading for an answer to some prayer, which if we could see and know all, we would not for worlds have granted to us. We may be unconsciously pleading for a curse instead of a blessing. I recollect reading a story which I almost shrink from repeating, it is so awful, but which so vividly illustrates this point that toning down many of its more shocking features, I shall venture to mention.

A mother had an only child—a boy—a dear, bright-eyed infant, her darling and her delight. God touched her little one, her only one, and laid him on a sick bed. Hour by hour the terrible fever raged, consuming bit by bit the precious life tissue, till at length it became clear to all that death was drawing near. Most earnest, most frequent had been that mother's prayers. How could she give up her only son? She wrestled with a vehemence which would take no denial. So intense was the violence of those prayers that one of her friends expostulated with her, on the want of resignation to a better wisdom, and fonder love than that of man. But remonstrance was in vain, and the strong pleadings of that mother prevailed. The tide of fever and of death rolled back from flushed face and beaded brow. Her darling was spared to her ; but ere she died she had learned to unpray that prayer, as she saw the child she would not let God take, go down the dark steps of persevering crime to the depths of ignominy and a death of shame. Oh may He give us earnestness indeed in prayer, but a spirit of more holy reliance upon Him that He will grant us the prayers we would *wish* to pray, even while He leaves those we have prayed unanswered.

(3.) *Inconsistency with a greater good.* Another reason for unanswered prayer is to be found in the inconsistency between our prayers and God's better purposes of wisdom towards others. The unanswered prayer of Moses will illustrate this. It was a bitter blow which kept Moses from entering in with Israel into the land of promise. So bravely he had defended them, so patiently he had toiled for them, so earnestly he had prayed and interceded for them, surely he might well expect to enter in. But that little sin excludes him. He prays,—he who had obtained in his intercession the turning away of God's wrath from Israel—he who had stood before them in the gap, prays now for himself that he may go across and see the glorious land. "But the Lord would not hear me," he says, and why? Not altogether as a punishment for that little sin, but because the granting of that prayer would have been inconsistent with the grand system of moral teaching by which God was educating Israel. This inconsistency between the prayer and the Diviner purposes of God's wisdom to Israel he speaks of, as the reason for its denial: "The Lord was angry with me *for your sakes*. The Lord would not hear me."

And that prayer of Gethsemane: "If it be possible,"—breathed in the perfection of holiness and resignation, could not be granted; for "thus it was written, and thus it behoved Christ to suffer." There is mystery in that prayer; but somehow the redemption of us unworthy was bound up with its denial.

Such are some of the causes and reasons of unanswered prayer. Let them teach us wisdom, resignation, trust, and patience. Let them lead us to look deep into our hearts, lest some root of bitterness, some deadly stem of long-hugged sin, some deceitful branch of unconscious insincerity be hindering the answers to our prayers. Let us realize, more and more, that no prayer of ours is either unwisely or unkindly left unanswered. Let us not despond, because we hear not His voice at all times. Let us call to mind that not we alone have been thus exercised with the discipline of prayer denied.

> "Let faith each weak petition fill,
> And waft it to the skies;
> And teach our hearts 'tis goodness still
> That grants it, or denies."

III. Lastly, we point to some of the *consolations*. There are many comforting thoughts respecting unanswered prayer. We shall briefly touch upon three of these:

(1.) There is often a heart-blessing given in an unanswered prayer.

This St. Paul found. The thorn was left to try to humble him; but the heart-blessing came, "My grace is sufficient for thee." Our Master in agony pleads that the cup might pass away from Him. The actual prayer is not granted. He drinks up the cup of sorrow which His Father gives Him. But the angel appears, strengthening Him. We may well believe that if we shall not be tempted above that we are able, the way to escape which does not come in the removal of the temptation will be sent in the heart-grace which makes us strong to bear it, or invincible to triumph over it.

(2.) God sometimes answers the heart's desires, though He denies the request of our lips. The Psalmist spoke of the wonderful mercy of God which had granted Him both —fulfilling the heart's desire, and not denying the request of His lips. But it is not always so. The request of the lips is left unanswered; but it is faulty faith to say that the heart's desire is overlooked; nay, it seems almost unalterably true, if we understand the expression in its truest, deepest meaning, that God WILL fulfil the desire of them that fear Him.

The fact is that our prayers often shape themselves into a form which not only asks a blessing, but suggests the channel through which the blessing should come. Now, if the blessing does come, and come through that channel, both the heart's desire and the request of the lips are fulfilled; but if the blessing comes through another channel, totally opposite from that suggested in the petition, yet the heart's desire is fulfilled. An incident is mentioned in a valuable book * by a living clergyman, which illustrates this truth.

* '*Christian Consolation,*' by Rev. D. Moore.

A servant of God was deeply tried at home in the way most painful for a child of God to be tried, in the open ungodliness of his own children. Long his prayers had gone up to God with strong crying and tears on their behalf; still and long they remained unanswered. At length the man of God was smitten with death sickness; and he prayed that that which God had not given him in answer to his prayers in life, might be granted to him at his death,—that a joyful and abundant entrance into the kingdom of God's dear Son would be vouchsafed to him, and that the sight of the Christian triumphing in and over death might be blessed to the conversion of his children. The sickness increased, the lull before death came. The sons and daughters of that man of God were around his bed, when lo! instead of the smile of triumph upon the face of the dying Christian, there was the sadness of despondency; instead of the shout of triumph on his lips, there was the cry of deep heart-misgiving. In doubt, and dark clouds of shadowed faith, that man of God passed away. But his prayer was answered, though the channel of blessing was changed. Those men and women seeing their father, that man of God, the man of blameless life, consistent Christianity, earnest faith and prayer, pass away in the throes of such tremendous heart-conflict, caught a glimpse of the terrors of the Lord, and foresaw how dense and unredeemed by hope must their own closing hours be! And this conviction brought their hearts to know their father's Saviour to be theirs, the strong Friend who could walk with them through the valley of the shadow of death, however dark it might be.

Prayers may be answered, while petitions are denied; and answers to prayer may be delayed till after we are gone. Doubt not then, my brother and sister, that many now unknown answers to prayer will troop forth to meet us at the gates of Paradise.

(3.) Lastly, there is a comfort in the

thought that there is one blessing which the most complete denial of our prayers cannot rob us of. Prayer may be answered—in whole or in part—delayed or denied; but whichever it be, we have this joy—and it is a real one—we have made known our requests to Him. We have laid our sorrows and wants at His feet. Come what may in the way of answer, we have told Him. Oh! it is no fancied delight, but a very real one, to tell Him all—to tell Him who is strong, that we are weak—even though He bid us bear our burden still,—to tell Him who is our exceeding joy, of our sorrows—even though He let us weep,—to tell Him who is wisdom, of our perplexities,—though He bid us wait and trust.

> "Oh, not a joy or blessing
> With this can we compare;
> The power that He has given us
> To pour our wants in prayer."

VII.

Barrenness in Prayer.

"Go with pure heart and feeling,
　Fling earthly thoughts away;
And in thy chamber kneeling,
　Do thou in secret pray."

ALMIGHTY God, the fountain of all wisdom, who knowest our necessities before we ask, and our ignorance in asking; We beseech Thee to have compassion upon our infirmities; and those things, which for our unworthiness we dare not, and for our blindness we cannot ask, vouchsafe to give us, for the worthiness of Thy Son Jesus Christ our Lord.
Amen.

Barrenness in Prayer.

There are, no doubt, many who have experienced at times an intense dissatisfaction with their prayers. They seem so lame, so cold, so profitless, till you are inclined to exclaim, "What a weariness, what a mockery it is!" You are constantly disappointed with yourselves. The heart that seemed so full has run empty ere you reached your knees. You have nothing to say; all your thoughts have fled from you; and the intense longing comes across your heart that some one would teach you how to pray.

I think the apostles experienced a measure of the feeling, or rather want of feeling, which has troubled you. I think it was some such sense of dissatisfaction which stole into their hearts at that moment, and prompted the petition,—"Lord, teach us to pray." The sight of their praying Master doubtless aroused the feeling. As they saw His earnestness, His faith, and how many things He had to lay before His Father, they craved to know the secret of that spirit of prayer. They contrasted it, in their own minds, with their own faint, dead, spiritless, and meagre petitions; and realized, with a vividness they never felt before, how grievously defective in all the features of true prayer were their own lifeless supplications.

And we have felt the same. Even without the opportunity the disciples had of hearing Christ pray, we have experienced this deep heart dissatisfaction, I trust, and have found ourselves longing that some one would teach us "how to pray." I do not pretend to supply the want here indicated; but I feel that it would be wrong not to touch upon what appear to me to be some of the causes of this trying sense of barrenness in prayer. I shall venture to touch upon three of these

—though doubtless there are many more—viz. Self-conceit, Self-ignorance, and Selfishness.

'I. *Self-conceit.*—We are very slow to learn the lesson of our own utter inability. Pride is a very dull scholar in the school of experience; and often and often she will beat about, seeking for every possible excuse for the failure of which she herself is the sole cause. We feel at some time, perhaps, that our hearts are prompted by an earnest desire to pray. We grow keenly alive for the moment to our own wants; but when we attempt to pray, we find the edge of that sense of need is gone. The heart appeared full, but when we knelt we found it empty. Like Tantalus of old, we anticipated a rich draught of the brimming flood; but as we stooped to drink it, it was gone. Vexed and disappointed we murmur at our privation, but are too blind to see its cause. We cannot see that our own self-conceit lies at the root of our failure. We thought we could do it of ourselves,—we anticipated rich heart communion; but we were miserably mistaken, because we did not realize that we are not sufficient of ourselves to think anything as of ourselves, but that our whole sufficiency is of God. We forgot that it is ever true, and must continue to be the heart experience of all the sons of God till the end of time, that we know not what we should pray for as we ought. We forgot that, for real successful prayer, a Divine energy of prayer must quicken our hearts; that the Holy Spirit of God must help our infirmities, making intercession for us with groanings which cannot be uttered.

This is one cause—a very chief cause, as I venture to believe—of barrenness in prayer. For though over and over again we acknowledge this truth; though we confess that we "have no power of ourselves to help ourselves;" that God's Holy Spirit must in all things direct and rule our hearts; yet the old spirit of self-conceit weaves her swift-spun web across our hearts, and beguiles us into the snare.

But this very discovery at once presents us with a remedy for barrenness in prayer; for, if we are disappointed that subjects of prayer have vexatiously failed us, here is the one grand thing for which we should pray— the gift of the Holy Spirit. This is the very dawn of spiritual light, the very threshold of prayer. For this blessing we shall not stand long knocking and pleading; since the clearest, brightest promise in all God's Book is this: "If ye, being evil, know how to give good gifts unto your children, how much more shall not My Father which is in heaven give the Holy Spirit to them that ask Him."

II. *Self-ignorance.*—There is a self-ignorance which causes barrenness and disappointment in prayer. There is, of course, a self-ignorance, and by consequence an ignorance of God (for he that knows not himself, how shall he know God) which begets fluency. Indeed, it is easy for ignorance to be fluent. Small and shallow minds fume much and flow fast; and there is a class of self-ignorants whose prayers run as rapidly from their supple lips as they rise easily from their shallow hearts. There are self-deceivers, who think that they shall be heard for their much speaking—who think that God's blessing is the *reward* of fine prayers. They do not realize prayer as a privilege too vast to be trifled with, and a pleasure too intense to be thrown away in empty words; but they link their salvation to their prayers, and depend on their many petitions for heaven. But these are not the class I speak of; for such are not aware of any barrenness in prayer. They live in a dream of self-delusion, and think they are eating and drinking; but a terrible awakening of heart hunger will be theirs sooner or later.

The class I speak of are those who are fully and bitterly aware of this barrenness in prayer, but who cannot quite trace the cause to their ignorance of themselves. But that they are very ignorant of themselves is, or ought to be, very plain. The very meagreness that they lament in their prayers might show it to them. For what are their prayers? They tell God that they have sinned, that they have grievously broken His commandments: they ask God to give them true repentance, and to forgive them for Jesus Christ's sake. Such, with very slight variations, might be taken as a type-prayer of the class of which I speak. But is it not a very good prayer? Yes, doubtless, good as far as it goes; but if that is all, it exhibits a very grievous amount of self-ignorance. The prayer might be from a certain heart a true and noble expression of spiritual longing; but with the persons to whom we allude this prayer is the stereotyped plate from which all their prayers for themselves, morning and evening, are struck off. With very little variation, and in the most conventional way—though, perhaps, with very real desire—they confess that they are sinners, unworthy and polluted; but there is not the confession of a single definite sin, or if there is, it is perhaps the result of some very rare circumstance which has impressed some special transgression more vividly upon their minds.

This habit of general confession is a fertile source of self-ignorance, besides being a fatal nurse of pride. It is an easy thing to confess that we are sinners, or that we are sinful; because it is only an inclusive confession in which our own individual guilt is lost sight of in the universal sinfulness of the race. Or even when we make our confession individual, and say, "Lord, I confess that I am sinful," yet in this kind of loose, general acknowledgment, the full force of the sinfulness of our many sins is not felt. To realize this, we must adopt a more particular mode of dealing with our own hearts, taking them to task; and recalling each special sin, and confessing it before God. Indeed it does argue a somewhat blunted spirituality when, at least in some measure, this is not done. The true, sensitive heart is uneasy till it has acknowledged its sin. The loving child feels burdened and uncomfortable till it has told its Father all. David experienced this. While he kept silence, and left his sin —mark, it was a particular sin—unconfessed, his bones waxed old through his roaring all the day long. Day and night God's hand was heavy upon him; and his moisture was like the drought in summer. All the freshness and the freedom of his spirit were gone; the dewdrops were shaken off his heart; till the sin was confessed—"this evil in Thy sight," as he calls it in another psalm; and then he experienced the fulness of the joy of a heart forgiven. Blessed, O! how "blessed is he whose transgression is forgiven, whose sin is covered," Psa. xxxii. 1.

The imitation of this practice,—the cultivation of that spirit which feels disquieted at the possession of a sin unconfessed to God—will greatly aid us in knowledge of ourselves. We shall gain a deeper, clearer insight into the dark recesses of our own hearts; and though, doubtless, we shall be filled with fear and amazement at the discoveries of our own vileness, yet we are taking the right step to promote our own peace, and pursue the pathway of holiness; for we are gaining a knowledge of our own need, which will supply us with abundant materials for our prayers. While we do this, though we may be much discouraged and cast down by reason of our sins, we shall not, I think, have reason to complain of barrenness in prayer, or to lament that we have nothing to say, nothing to ask. Oh! may we realize this, and echo the prayer of the Psalmist for this deep self-knowledge. "Search me, O God, and try the very ground of my heart, and see if there be any wicked way in me, and lead me in the way everlasting."

III. *Selfishness in prayer.*—Perhaps subordinate to the two we have spoken of, but certainly more or less connected with them, and influencing them, a spirit of selfishness in prayer will lead to the sense of barrenness. By selfishness in prayer, I mean that spirit in prayer which confines all our supplications to our own individual need. I do not mean that we do not include by name many of our friends and relatives within the circle of our prayers. Of course we all of us do this. But even when we do so, is it not often done in a perfunctory way? Is not the spirit which yearns over them very far removed from us? Is there the presence of that feeling of the apostle, who described himself as travailing in birthpangs for those in whose hearts he desired to see Christ formed. And often God visits us with barrenness because we fail to grow in heart-sympathy and Christian longing for the welfare of others. It is the very law of Christ that His love should spread, as it is the law of hydrostatics that pressure should circulate in all directions through a volume of water; and when we in a niggardly forgetfulness of others violate that law, we are met with the punishment of a straitening in ourselves.

Nor is it less a privilege than a law. What privilege greater than this, that we should ask, and God should give us life for them that sin not unto death. It is a privilege which God's children in all ages have joyously embraced: Abraham interceding for Lot; Moses for Israel; the church at Jerusalem for the imprisoned apostle. It is the privilege which Christian ministers have besought their people to make use of for *them.* "Brethren, pray for us," is the language not of St. Paul only, but of every labourer for Christ who knows his deep necessities. It is a privilege which Christ has not forgotten on behalf of us the wayfarers and pilgrims in this wilderness world,—seeing "He ever liveth to make intercession for us."

VIII

Regularity in Prayer.

"Or if 'tis e'er denied thee
   In solitude to pray,
Should holy thoughts come o'er thee,
   When friends are round thy way;
Even then the silent breathing
   Of thy spirit raised above,
Shall reach His throne of glory,
   Who is Mercy, Truth, and Love."

O ALMIGHTY GOD, who alone canst order the unruly wills and affections of sinful men; Grant unto Thy people, that they may love the thing which Thou commandest, and desire that which Thou dost promise; that so, among the sundry and manifold changes of the world, our hearts may surely there be fixed, where true joys are to be found; through Jesus Christ our Lord. *Amen.*

Regularity in Prayer.

More joy is often desired by Christ's people, who do not learn to pray more. Spiritual joy in Christ is the product of our prayer and God's answer. The heart is happy whose wishes are fulfilled. Turn your wishes into prayers, and be glad evermore. A quiet heart is said to be a perpetual feast. Communion with God causes that quietude which is the repast of the spirit. The heart that would rejoice must learn to pray. The apostle who bids us "Rejoice evermore," immediately adds "Pray without ceasing" (1 Thes. v. 17). The word of promise from the Prophet's lips was similar: "I will make them joyful in my house of prayer!"

If we complain of hearts sad and spirits

dull, and unable to joy in God, it may be that the feebleness, timidity, or irregularity of our prayers have occasioned this deadness. Unknown or unrealized by us, our spirits are perhaps languishing for the very atmosphere of prayer, and will not, cannot be satisfied with any blessings or pleasures, however sweet or tempting; as the caged bird turns away from the daintiest crumb, because it is pining for the bright, clear air of its warm, sunny home.

If, then, if you would rejoice, pray. If you would rejoice evermore, pray without ceasing. There are three practical thoughts which may be associated with this precept.

(1.) *Cultivate a constantly prayerful spirit.*— There is a spirit, which is ever recognizing its own need, and Christ's presence. A prayerfulness pervades such a spirit at all times, and tinges all its actions with the triple hues of humility, faith, and love. The act of prayer cannot be continuous; but the spirit of prayer should breathe through every word and work. The fragrance of it may sweeten and freshen every act, as the perfume of flowers lingers in the air when the flowers themselves are gone.

(2.) *Seize opportunities of prayer.*—A prayerful spirit gains many an opportunity for silent and happy communion with God, which a prayerless spirit loses. When an indolent Christian complains of interruptions, constant difficulties, and vexatious hindrances, which prevent the frequency and deaden the fervour of his prayers, the vigilant and prayerful spirited child of God finds abundant and precious opportunities of pouring out his needs and telling his difficulties to the Friend who hears at all times.

By the roadside, the peasant as he trudges to his fields of toil, the clear fresh morning air fanning his cheeks, and the glad carol of the birds raining music from the sky—the hard-worked servant girl as she goes about her early morning work in the dull murky light of a city dawn—the business man as he threads through the rising roar of the street-traffic to his daily business,—these, if their hearts are with Him, will often find Him with their hearts; and their wishes and pains, their hopes and fears will be laid before Him in the sweet little intervals of every-day work, which thus become green places in the dreary desert of daily drudgery.

(3.) *Be regular in prayer.*—A prayerful spirit, jealously seizing on little occasional opportunities of prayer, will never let these take the place of regular and stated times of supplication. "At morning, and at evening, and at noon-day," the Psalmist sought retirement for communion with God. With too many of us, the midday hour is too full of work to admit of our setting apart a short time for such a pleasure; but with some we fear the opportunity which a midday leisure gives is not seized upon for prayer. But whatever your occupation may be, never be satisfied with mere prayerful ejaculations, as substitutes for stated times for meditation and prayer. There is a temptation even to the most Christ-loving to omit the duty of keeping resolutely to some fixed times of prayer, in the tranquil enjoyment of heart communion with God. We think that at any time we may turn our thoughts and desires after Him; but the idea is one which will soon disprove itself, when we find that the prayerful spirit forsakes us since we have forsaken the morning and evening times of prayer. "Pray without ceasing" at least enjoins upon us regularity in prayer.

For our guidance at these regular times of prayer, the following two thoughts may be found useful:

(a.) *Seek to be alone when you pray.*—Our Master often sought out a solitary place for prayer. He taught us to do the same. "Pray to thy Father in secret;" and He gave us minute instruction to secure ourselves from distraction, and even the apprehension of interruption: "Enter into thy closet, and when thou hast shut thy door, pray to thy Father which is in secret, and thy Father which seeth in secret, shall reward thee openly." The surface of the canal is fretted as long as the sluice-gate is open, and the stream of water flows through; and neither can the spirit reach true tranquillity as long as the inflow of worldly thoughts and cares is suffered to rush in upon it. We must close the door of the heart upon all these; and to do this we need to shut out all those suggestive associations which stir the mind with the memory of care. We must be alone. But this is not enough for some minds. There are some natures so constituted that the very faintest apprehension of interruption completely destroys the possibility of earnest and real thought; and, with most, prayer is enfeebled where the mind is fearing an intrusion, and all the outer senses are on the alert to catch the approaching footstep of the intruder. This painful state of apprehensiveness distracts the mind from its purpose, and opens the avenues of a hundred wandering thoughts. Attention and interest flag; ardour cools; faith droops; and prayer degenerates into the hasty recitation of a few familiar phrases. It is a most wise and loving word of Christ, showing how much He knows our frail and halting hearts, which bids us when we pray to enter into our chamber, and shut to the door.

(*b.*) *Avoid desultoriness in your prayers.*—Vague wishes and pointless petitions can scarcely win a blessing. Success will be found to depend very much on the distinctness of the object sought. A man of great ambition can hardly avoid disappointment if he has no definite purpose of life in view. The same is true of prayer. A desultory accumulation of undigested and ill-considered desires will result in a feeling of weariness rather than refreshment. The spirit will have exhausted itself with the boundlessness of the range of its petitions, and will hardly know where to look for an answer. We may indeed ask much in prayer; and to a spirit quickened by real desire and sense of need, there will be many wants to be made known, and many shortcomings to deplore; but there will not be an indefiniteness, but reality and distinctness in such prayers.

Christ's own teaching will help us here. "After this manner pray ye," He said; and saying it, He gave us a prayer full of point, simplicity, and earnestness. The order is clear, and each petition is definite but comprehensive. The greater subjects, those which all His people are interested in, are taken first,—the individual and temporal needs come afterwards. The child who goes to pray to his Father in Heaven, first prays for those successes which the member of the celestial family, the citizen of the heavenly kingdom, and the patriot of the world, naturally holds dearest and highest. "Hallowed be Thy name. Thy kingdom come. Thy will be done on earth, as it is in heaven." His foremost attention is to these; for to promote these ends he is enrolled in the army of Christ, and all personal peace and good fortune are but secondary, since self is lost in service.

But he has distinct and great petitions to offer for himself,—wants which are daily felt, and which he knows will be daily supplied. There is no vagueness in this prayer: "Give us this day our daily bread;" for the very comprehensiveness of it points to the necessity of which we are most sensible. Whatever be the need of which you are keenly aware, *that* you may mention; only be sure that you understand it as a *need*. Be not content to pray for "strength" or for "grace;" but try to realize the particular need for which that strength is required, for "grace to help" is promised for "every time of need."

You can trace the same definiteness in the next clause: "Forgive us our trespasses."

All have sins to be forgiven. The holiest need daily to wash their feet; but how many suffer a vague phrase to cover over many a particular sin which should be distinctly realized, and bewailed and repented of as a sin. The second part of the clause is fitted to call forth the recollection of a very commonly forgotten class of sin. "As we forgive them that trespass against us." Who can use this petition, or pray after this manner, without feeling often very sharply the prickings of self-reproach, as the names of some alienated friend, or some associate of whose fault we cherish an exaggerated remembrance, recur to our minds? The language "as we forgive" brings conviction to many of our hearts that we have not done all we could to manifest good-will, to remove misapprehension,— that our forgiveness has been a lame and stiff thing, most unlike the wise and ungrudging forgiveness of God. He melts away the cloud of sin which we placed between our hearts and Him. Have we tried to get rid of the cloud in our hearts which dulls affection towards a brother? Have we striven, by kindness or generous forgetfulness, to dissipate the cloud which chills their hearts' love to us? It will not do for us to let these questionings and convictions die. We must distinctly recognize the shortcoming, and definitely set ourselves to pray against it, and to forsake it. The recognition of these faults and sins is painful; but better far is this pain, than a shallow and false ease of mind. The pain of seeing wherein we have failed and fallen is an incentive and aid to amendment, and brings us that knowledge and experience of ourselves which are stepping-stones to the higher, holier, and happier life. But this insight into our infirmities and sins is never largely gained when we content ourselves with vague and desultory prayers.

These hints and thoughts are chiefly designed to lead to some reflection upon the great value of method in our prayers. Mere formality chokes devotion; but true system aids it. Constancy and perseverance in prayer is stimulated by the observance of some few rules, which careful self-examination and heart-watchfulness have suggested; for thus we can note from time to time our progress, check our short-comings, survey our conduct, and glean that self-knowledge which compels us in every thing by prayer and supplication with thanksgiving to make known our requests to God (Phil. iv. 6).

IX.

𝕸𝖊𝖉𝖎𝖙𝖆𝖙𝖎𝖔𝖓𝖘 𝖆𝖓𝖉 𝕻𝖗𝖆𝖞𝖊𝖗𝖘.

"My meditation of Him shall be sweet."
Psa. civ. 34.

"Let the words of my mouth, and the meditation of my heart, be alway acceptable in Thy sight, O Lord, my strength, and my redeemer."

Psa. xix. 14.

Meditations and Prayers
For a Week.

MONDAY.

The Love of God.

"God so loved the world, that He gave His only begotten Son, that whosoever believeth in Him should not perish, but have everlasting life."

God loved the world! How different is God's thought towards man from man's of God! My unbelieving heart whispers, God loves me not: blessed, thrice blessed, is this word of Thine, O Father, to contradict the whispered doubt. But what is there in me that God should love? Nay, that I know not; but that He made me, and His nature is to love all that He has made. I know not, but that He spared not His own Son.

But there is nothing in me worthy of His love! Yes, that I know, but that unworthiness commends to me that His love is true. "God commendeth His love toward us, in that, while we were yet sinners, Christ died for us."

But I shall tire out His love with my constant failures and faithlessness! Nay, what shall separate from the love of Christ? He that gave up His Son will give me freely all things that I need.

Prayer.

O FATHER of mercies—God of love—let not the voice of the tempter, or the whispers of doubt darken Thy promise to my soul, or drive me from Thy side! Help me to cleave ever to Thy word, and find in it an assurance sufficient to silence the voice of the enemy. Forgive my distrust, and help my unbelief. Shed abroad Thy love in my soul by Thy Holy Spirit; for the sake of Him in whom Thou hast made known Thy love, Jesus Christ, our Lord. Amen.

'Tis not alone because Thy names of Wisdom,
    Power, and Love,   [skies above;
Are written on the earth beneath, and the glorious
We praise Thee, Lord, for these; yet not for these
    alone   [throne.
The incense of a Christian's love arises to Thy
We love Thee, Lord, because, when we had erred
    and gone astray,   [ward way;
Thou didst recall our wand'ring souls into the heaven-
When helpless, hopeless, we were lost in sin and
    sorrow's night,
Thou didst beam forth a guiding ray of Thy benignant
    light.

Because when we forsook Thy ways, nor kept Thy
    holy will,
Thou wert not an avenging Judge, but a gracious
    Father still;
Because we have forgotten Thee, but Thou hast not
    forgot,—   [not.
Because we have forsaken Thee, but Thou forsakest
Because, O Lord! Thou lovedst us with everlasting
    love;
Because Thou gav'st Thy Son to die that we might
    live above;
Because when we were doomed to hell, Thou gav'st
    the hope of heaven,
We love because we much have sinned, and much
    have been forgiven.

J. A. Elliott.

TUESDAY.

The Sufferings of Christ.

O MY soul! consider the things which thy Saviour has suffered for thy sake. He was despised and rejected of men, a Man of sorrows, and acquainted with grief. He had not where to lay His head. His brethren did not believe in Him. He endured the contradiction of sinners against Himself. His life was continually in His hand. They gathered together, and took counsel to take away His life. He was troubled in spirit. He was in an agony, and His sweat was as it were great drops of blood. He was betrayed, forsaken, and denied. His face was marred more than the sons of men! They plaited a crown of thorns, and placed it on His head. They crucified Him; and the thieves that were crucified with Him reviled Him. They gave Him gall for meat, and when He was thirsty they gave Him vinegar to drink. They pierced His side, and there came out blood and water. Was ever sorrow like unto His sorrow? It was sorrow for thee, my soul, He suffered thus for thee. Hearken! "Surely He hath borne our griefs, and carried our sorrows. He was wounded for our transgressions, He was bruised for our iniquities: the chastisement of our peace was upon Him; and with His stripes we are healed." "He bare our sins in His own Body on the tree."

Prayer.

O Thou scourged, forsaken, and crucified Christ! O suffering and rejected Saviour! pardon my long negligence of Thy love, and my indifference to Thee! Surely, by Thy cross and passion, Thou hast redeemed my soul! Thy blood, O bleeding Lamb of God, cleanses from all sin! Let not Thy toil and anguish be in vain; but pity, spare, and save Thy servant, whom Thou hast redeemed. Hear, for Thy mercy's sake! Jesus, hear and save!

Birds have their quiet nest,
Foxes their holes, and man his peaceful bed;
All creatures have their rest,—
But Jesus had not where to lay His head.

And yet He came to give
The weary, heavy-laden, rest;
To bid the sinner live,
And soothe our griefs to slumber on His breast.

Why then am I, my God,
Permitted thus the path of peace to tread?
Peace purchased by the Blood
Of Him who had not where to lay His head.

I who once made Him grieve,
I who once bid His gentle spirit mourn,
Whose hand assayed to weave,
For His meek brow, the cruel crown of thorns.

Yes, but for pardoning grace,
I feel I never should in glory see
The brightness of that face,
That once was pale and agonized for me.

Let the birds seek their nests,
Foxes their holes, and men their peaceful bed;
Come, Saviour, on my breast,
Deign to repose Thine oft-rejected Head.

J. S. B. Monsell.

WEDNESDAY.

The Might of the Saviour.

"ALL power is given unto Me in heaven and earth."

"Greater is He that is with us, than he that is against us!"

"If God be for us, who can be against us?"

"No man is able to pluck them out of My Father's Hand."

Yea! Thou art great and Thou art good, and "who is he that can deliver after this sort?"

But thy sins are great and strong, and they are fast bound and interwoven with the wishes of thy heart, and the thoughts of thy mind!—Yes, O tempter, my sins are great and subtle and strong; but my Saviour hath curbed the sea—hath loosed those whom the tyrant bowed down in his bonds—hath forgiven the sinful—hath given us the victory over the sting of death and the strength of sin.

But time is long—the world is bewildering, and thy faith is small.—Yes, O tempter, my faith is but small; but my faith saves me not. He saves me on whom my faith is fixed; and He in the midst of me is mighty. The world, I know, is ensnaring; but He bade me be of good cheer, for He had overcome the world. Time and life are long to the feeble in strength, and wear out the firmest courage; but though these shall perish, He is eternal; His years fail not: He is the same for ever.

Prayer.

O MIGHTY Saviour, Sovereign of the worlds, and promised dweller in Thy people's hearts; be mighty in me against the tempter. Draw near, and of Thy mercy destroy the power of him who strives to vex my soul; for I am Thy servant—Thy child, relying on Thy mercy and Thy power. O rise and save me, for Thy great name's sake.

For a Week.

In weakness at Thy feet I lie,
   Thine eye each pang hath seen,
Scarce can I lift my heart on high,
   Yet, Lord, on Thee I lean.

Lean on Thy sure, unfailing Word,
   Thy gentle "It is I;"
For Thou, my ever-living Lord,
   Know'st what it is to die.

Thou wilt be with me when I go,—
   Thy life, my life in death;
For in the lowest depths, I know
   Thine Arms are underneath.

'Tis not the infant's feeble grasp
   Which holds the mother fast;
It is the mother's gentle clasp
   Around her darling cast.

Just so Thy child would cling to Thee,
   Knowing Thy pity long;
For feeble as my faith may be,
   The Hand I clasp is strong.

A. L. Waring.

THURSDAY.

The Holy Spirit.

"THE love of God is shed abroad in our hearts by the Holy Ghost, which is given unto us."

"God hath sent forth the Spirit of His Son into your hearts, crying, Abba, Father."

Sweet and soul-comforting is that thought — The Holy Ghost is given — Christ is glorified. The Spirit is poured out from on high. There is no need of hopelessness in the great conflict with sin and evil. A power is vouchsafed to us strong against all evil and over every sin. This power is the Holy Spirit—the Lord and Life-giver. He can give life to the soul, and teach that love which it is heart-life to know. He can enable me to realize the Father's care and rule. "This is life eternal, to know Thee, the only true God, and Jesus Christ whom Thou hast sent." The Holy Spirit will reveal this knowledge more fully to my heart.

Behold! I know not what to ask, or how to pray for it as I ought; but the Heavenly Spirit will help mine infirmities,—will make intercession with me, and for me, according to the will of God! By Him let me be led in life and in prayer.

Prayer.

O LOVING Spirit, lead me forth in the ways of holiness, and into the land of righteousness. Subdue within me unholy affections, and selfish imaginations. Aid me to curb my own will. Teach me to do my great Father's will: help me to delight in doing it. Make my heart the temple of Thy perpetual abode. Leave me not, neither forsake me; but be Thou ever with me, the Spring and Fountain of eternal peace and purity. Bring all helpful and holy recollections to my mind. Fill me with happy thoughts of my Saviour and my Eternal Home,—for the sake of Jesus Christ, with Thee and the Father one God. Amen.

"Sweet is the solace of Thy love,
　My heavenly Friend, to me,
While through the hidden way of faith
　I journey home with Thee,
Learning by quiet thankfulness
　As a dear child to be.

"Oft in a dark and lonely place,
　I hush my hasten'd breath,
To hear the comfortable words
　Thy loving Spirit saith;
And feel my safety in Thy hand
　From every kind of death.

"No other comforter I need,
　If Thou, O Lord, be mine;—
Thy rod will bring my spirit low,
　Thy fire my heart refine,
And cause me pain that none can heal
　By other love than Thine.

"Still in the solitary place
　I would awhile abide,
Till with the solace of Thy love
　My heart is satisfied,
And all my hopes of happiness
　Stay calmly at Thy side."

FRIDAY.

Peace.

"My peace I give unto you: not as the world giveth, give I unto you. Let not your heart be troubled, neither let it be afraid." "Great peace have they that love Thy law, and nothing shall offend them." "The peace of God, which passeth understanding, shall keep your hearts and minds through Christ Jesus."

Yea! O blessed Saviour, Thou hast made peace by the blood of Thy cross. Justified by faith we have peace with Thee! But why art thou cast down, O my soul; and why so disquieted within! Are not thy sins forgiven thee for His name's sake? Did He not speak peace to the far-off, as well as to the near? Is He not faithful that promised? Have we not boldness to draw near, through the blood of Jesus? Why, then, art thou cast down, O my soul? He has made peace, I know;

but I have not that peace which flows like a river. I trust to Him, in whom I find all my need supplied; but I am not fully at rest. I am as one who, though at anchor, is yet rolling about among the stormy waves. The cable is strong, and will not fail; but I am weary and tempest-tossed. Christ, my Saviour, will not fail me; but I am full of deep unrest!

But hearken! Christ has made peace; but He is more than Peace-maker: He is thy peace. Look not at the storm, but look to Him. Receive Him, and thou shalt immediately be in the haven of rest.

Prayer.

To Thee, O Jesus, Thou Peace of the troubled heart, I come! Save me from myself. Shine into my heart with Thy light and love. Melt away all cold distrust. Take away all sin; and make me like to Thyself, for Thy love and kindness' sake, O Lord! Amen.

O'er many a weary mile,
   And lonesome way, My child must roam,
Far from the welcome smile
   Of her own happy Home,—
      Through many a scene
      Of brighter green,—
Yet oft she'll wish she had the swallow's wing,
Back to the one loved spot her longing soul to bring.

There is but one sure Home
   Where peace is ever found;
Whose links, where'er you roam,
   Can never be unbound.
      It is the rest
      Of spirits blest,
When from the world they turn in Him to dwell
Whose holy peace alone its bitter strife can quell.

Seek, then, that Home of peace!
   Its charms how pure they shine!
Its love shall never cease,
   No death its links untwine.
      Oh, make your nest
      On His true breast,
Whose love will light this dark and dreary way,
And still shine more and more unto the perfect day.

Evans.

SATURDAY.

Death.

ALL must die! Thou, too, O my soul's guest—thou frail body—thou must turn to dust, and all thy thoughts and schemes and resolves must then perish. Nay, the thoughts that are born of God cannot die. My thoughts outrun my life, and outlive my death, when my affections are on things above—where Christ my Master sitteth.

But the taking down of the tabernacle is painful; the passage from this world to the other is dark, and the river of death is deep and cold; and the further bank lies in a cloudy distance; and thou must go forth alone! Nay, not alone. Though I walk through the valley of the shadow of death, Thou, O Shepherd of my soul, art with me. Thou hast said: "I will never leave thee, nor forsake thee."

"It is appointed unto men once to die, but after that the judgment!" Who can stand the scrutiny of Him who is of purer eyes than to behold iniquity, and into whose presence nought that defileth shall enter? Who shall stand before His judgment seat? Nay, but who is He that condemneth, since Christ hath died, and hath risen again? Who shall gainsay His voice who intercedes at God's right hand?

Prayer.

O GOD, the true Life of all things,—who hast revealed Thy Son as the resurrection and the life,—enable me so to die to sin, and live to Thee, that I may die to fear, and live in hope of the perfect consummation and bliss, both of body and soul, in Thy eternal kingdom, for the sake of Jesus Christ our Lord. Amen.

My God! I know that I must die,
  My mortal life is passing hence;
On earth I neither hope nor try
  To find a lasting residence;
Then teach me, by Thy heavenly grace,
With joy and peace my death to face.

My God! I know not *when* I die,
  What is the moment or the hour,
How soon the clay may broken lie,
  How quickly pass away the flower;
Then may Thy child prepared be
Through time to meet eternity.

My God! I know not *how* I die,
  For death has many ways to come;
In dark, mysterious agony,
  Or gently, as in sleep, to some;
Just as Thou wilt! if but I be
For ever, blessed Lord, with Thee.

My gracious God! when I must die,
  Oh, bear my happy soul above,
With Christ, my Lord, eternally
  To share Thy glory and Thy love!
Then comes it right and well to me,
When, where, and how my death shall be.

B. Schmolk.
"*Hymns from the Land of Luther.*"

SUNDAY.

Heaven.

"There shall be no night there." Darkness shall cease. Ignorance shall end there, where we shall know as we are known. Doubt shall end, where God Himself shall be with us, and be our God. Sin shall end, where we shall be like Him, for we shall see Him as He is.

There shall be no more curse; for the reign of the bondage of corruption shall end; the thorns and briers will give place to the tree of life, with its abundant fruit and healing leaves; the glorious liberty of God's children will spread unhindered, for the Throne of God and of the Lamb will be there.

All things shall be new, and the former things will pass away; but though new, not strange nor unfamiliar will those new things be. The Voice that will welcome us there will be the Voice that called us near to Himself on earth. The many mansions are prepared for us by the Hands which were pierced for our sins.

Prayer.

O HELP me, Heavenly Father, who hast prepared such good things for them that love Thee, to live in the contemplation of Thee, that the sight of Thy paradise may be to me as the sight of home.. Help me so to contend against sin here that the holy peace of Heaven may be true joy to my heart. Help me to live and walk in Thy light here, that I may walk hereafter in the light of Thy Holy City, among the nations of them that are saved—through the mercy which Thou hast shown to us in Thy dear Son Jesus Christ, our Lord. Amen.

For a Week.

What no human eye hath seen,
   What no mortal ear hath heard,
What on thought hath never been,
   In its noblest flights, conferred, —
This hath God prepared in store
   For His people evermore.

When the shaded pilgrim land
   Fades before my closing eye,
Then, revealed on either hand,
   Heaven's own scenery shall lie;
Then the veil of flesh shall fall,
   Now concealing, darkening all!

Heavenly landscapes calmly bright,
   Life's pure river murmuring low,
Forms of loveliness and light,
   Lost to earth long time ago.
Yes, mine own, lamented long,
   Shines amid the angel throng.

Many a joyful sight was given,
   Many a lovely vision here,
Hill and vale, and starry even,
   Friendship's smile, affection's tear;
These were shadows sent in love
   Of realities above.

When upon my wearied ear
   Earth's last echoes faintly die,
Then shall angel harps draw near,
   All the chorus of the sky:
Long-hushed voices blend again
Sweetly in that welcome strain.

When this aching heart shall rest,
   All its busy pulses o'er,
From her mortal robes undrest,
   Shall my spirit upward soar.
Then shall unimagined joy
All my thoughts and powers employ.

Jesus reigns, the Life, the Sun
   Of that wondrous world above;
All the clouds and storms are gone,
   All is light and all is love.
All the shadows melt away
In the blaze of perfect day.

Lange.
"Hymns from the Land of Luther."

X.

Suggestive Outlines.

Those who pray have sins to confess—wants to tell—friends and acquaintances to pray for—mercies to be thankful for. Illustrations of these various divisions of prayer may be plentifully found in Scripture and elsewhere. But it may not be amiss to append in this concluding chapter suggestive passages, prayers, and hymns, illustrative of these divisions of prayer.

Some may find these useful as hints; and all may derive encouragement in their own prayers from noting the way in which their predecessors in the faith wrestled and wept in their prayers. But to none are they intended to be more than *suggestive;* for though we are all alike in need of prayer, yet all have needs which none but themselves can shape into prayer.

I.—CONFESSION.

"I will arise, and go to my father, and will say unto him, Father, I have sinned against heaven, and before thee, and am no more worthy to be called thy son."—*Luke* xv. 18, 19.

Read—Nehemiah i. 4-11; Psalm li.

Prayer.

Almighty God, Father of our Lord Jesus Christ, Maker of all things, Judge of all men; we acknowledge and bewail our manifold sins and wickedness, which we, from time to time, most grievously have committed, by thought, word, and deed, against Thy Divine Majesty, provoking most justly Thy wrath and indignation against us. We do earnestly repent, and are heartily sorry for these our misdoings; the remembrance of them is grievous unto us; the burden of them is intolerable. Have mercy upon us, have mercy upon us, most merciful Father; for Thy Son, our Lord Jesus Christ's sake, forgive us all that is past; and grant that we may ever hereafter serve and please Thee in newness of life, to the honour and glory of Thy name; through Jesus Christ our Lord. *Amen.*

> Lord, when we bend before Thy throne,
>   And our confessions pour,
> Teach us to feel the sins we own,
>   And hate what we deplore.
>
> Our broken spirits, pitying, see;
>   And penitence impart;
> And let a kindling glance from Thee
>   Beam hope upon the heart.
>
> When we disclose our wants in pray
>   May we our wills resign;
> And not a thought our bosom share
>   Which is not wholly Thine.
>
> Let faith each meek petition fill,
>   And waft it to the skies;
> And teach our hearts 'tis goodness still
>   That grants it, or denies.

CONFESSION.

"REND your heart, and not your garments, and turn unto the Lord your God; for He is gracious and merciful, slow to anger, and of great kindness, and repenteth Him of the evil."

Joel ii. 13.

READ—Daniel ix. 3-20; Psalm vi. 1-9.

Prayer.

O MOST mighty God, and merciful Father, who hast compassion upon all men, and hatest nothing that Thou hast made; who wouldest not the death of a sinner, but that he should rather turn from his sin, and be saved; mercifully forgive us our trespasses; receive and comfort us, who are grieved and wearied with the burden of our sins. Thy property is always to have mercy; to Thee only it appertaineth to forgive sins. Spare us, therefore, good Lord, spare Thy people, whom Thou hast redeemed; enter not into judgment with Thy servants, who are vile earth, and miserable sinners: but so turn Thine anger from us, who meekly acknowledge our vileness, and truly repent us of our faults, and so make haste to help us in this world, that we may ever live with Thee in the world to come; through Jesus Christ our Lord. *Amen.*

>WHEN at Thy footstool, Lord, I bend,
>   And plead with Thee for mercy there,
>Think of the sinner's dying Friend,
>   And for His sake receive my prayer.
>
>O think not of my shame and guilt,
>   My thousand stains of deepest dye;
>Think of the Blood which Jesus spilt,
>   And let that Blood my pardon buy.
>
>Think, Lord, how I am still Thine own,
>   The trembling creature of Thy hand;
>Think how my heart to sin is prone,
>   And what temptations round me stand.
>
>O think upon Thy Holy Word,
>   And every plighted promise there;
>How prayer should evermore be heard,
>   And how Thy glory is to spare.

II.—SUPPLICATION.

"WHATSOEVER ye shall ask in prayer, believing, ye shall receive." *Matt.* xxi. 22.

READ—Gen. xxxii. 9-12 and 24-31.
1 Sam. i. 9-19.
2 Kings xx. 2-12.
2 Chron. xiv. 9-14.

Prayer.

O GOD, merciful Father, that despisest not the sighing of a contrite heart, nor the desire of such as be sorrowful; mercifully assist our prayers that we make before Thee in all our troubles and adversities, whensoever they oppress us; and graciously hear us, that those evils, which the craft and subtilty of the devil or man worketh against us, be brought to nought; and by the providence of Thy goodness they may be dispersed; that we, Thy servants, being hurt by no persecutions, may evermore give thanks unto Thee in Thy holy Church; through Jesus Christ our Lord.

HAST thou a care for words too deep,
It chases from thine eyelids sleep?
To thy Redeemer take that care,
And change anxiety for prayer.

Hast thou a Hope, with which thy heart
Would almost feel it death to part?
Entreat thy God that hope to crown,
Or give thee strength to lay it down.

Whate'er the care that breaks thy rest,
Whate'er the wish that swells thy breast,
Spread before God that wish, that care,
And change anxiety for prayer.

SUPPLICATION.

"THEY shall call on My name, and I will hear them."
Zech. xiii. 9.

READ—Luke xi. 1-14.
Acts x. 1-9.
Acts xvi. 16-27.

Prayer.

O ALMIGHTY LORD, and everlasting God, vouchsafe, we beseech Thee, to direct, sanctify, and govern, both our hearts and bodies, in the ways of Thy laws, and in the works of Thy commandments; that through Thy most mighty protection, both here and ever, we may be preserved in body and soul; through our Lord and Saviour, Jesus Christ. *Amen.*

> O THOU, who driest the mourner's tear,
>   How dark this world would be,
> If, when deceived and wounded here,
>   We could not fly to Thee!
>
> But Thou wilt heal that broken heart,
>   Which, like the plants that throw
> Their fragrance from the wounded part,
>   Breathes sweetest out of woe.
>
> O! who could bear life's stormy doom,
>   Did not Thy wing of love
> Come brightly wafting through the gloom
>   Some peace-branch from above?
>
> Then sorrow, touch'd by Thee, grows bright
>   With more than rapture's ray;
> As darkness shows us worlds of light
>   We never saw by day.

III.—INTERCESSION.

"PRAYING always with all prayer and supplication in the Spirit, and watching thereunto with all perseverance and supplication for all saints." *Eph.* vi. 18.

READ—1 Tim. ii. 1-5; Acts xii. 1-18; Philemon 22.

Prayer.

O GOD, the Creator and Preserver of all mankind, we humbly beseech Thee for all sorts and conditions of men; that Thou wouldest be pleased to make Thy ways known unto them, Thy saving health unto all nations. More especially, we pray for the good estate of the Catholic Church; that it may be so guided and governed by Thy good Spirit, that all who profess and call themselves Christians may be led into the way of truth, and hold the faith in unity of spirit, in the bond of peace, and in righteousness of life. Finally, we commend to Thy fatherly goodness all those who are any ways afflicted, or distressed, in mind, body, or estate; that it may please Thee to comfort and relieve them, according to their several necessities, giving them patience under their sufferings, and a happy issue out of all their afflictions. And this we beg for Jesus Christ His sake. *Amen.*

O SAVIOUR Christ, our woes dispel;
  For some are sick and some are sad,
And some have never loved Thee well,
  And some have lost the love they had;

And some have found the world is vain,
  Yet from the world they break not free;
And some have friends who give them pain,
  Yet have not sought a friend in Thee.

And none, O Lord, have perfect rest,
  For none are wholly free from sin;
And they who fain would serve Thee best,
  Are conscious most of wrong within.

O Saviour Christ, Thou too art Man;
  Thou hast been troubled, tempted, tried;
Thy kind but searching glance can scan
  The very wounds that shame would hide.

Intercession.

"If any man see his brother sin a sin which is not unto death, he shall ask, and he shall give him life for them that sin not unto death." 1 *John* v. 16.

> Read—1 Kings xvii. 17-24.
> Matt. xviii. 15-20.
> James v. 15 to end.

Prayer.

O MERCIFUL GOD, who hast made all men, and hatest nothing that Thou hast made, nor wouldest the death of a sinner, but rather that he should be converted and live; have mercy upon all Jews, Turks, Infidels, and Heretics, and take from them all ignorance, hardness of heart, and contempt of Thy word; and so fetch them home, blessed Lord, to Thy flock, that they may be saved among the remnant of the true Israelites, and be made one fold under one Shepherd, through Jesus Christ our Lord, who liveth and reigneth with Thee and the Holy Spirit, one God, world without end. *Amen.*

> ABIDE with me from morn till eve,
> For without Thee I cannot live;
> Abide with me when night is nigh,
> For without Thee I dare not die.
>
> If some poor wandering child of Thine
> Have spurn'd to-day the Voice Divine,
> Now, Lord, the gracious work begin;
> Let him no more lie down in sin.
>
> Watch by the sick, enrich the poor
> With blessings from Thy boundless store:
> Be every mourner's sleep to-night,
> Like infant's slumbers, pure and light.

IV.—THANKSGIVING.

"BLESSED be the Lord, because He hath heard the voice of my supplications." *Psa.* xxviii. 6.

READ—1 Sam. i. 24 to end   Isa. xii.
Ezra iii. 10-13 ; Hos. xiv.

Prayer.

ALMIGHTY GOD, Father of all mercies, we, Thine unworthy servants, do give Thee most humble and hearty thanks for all Thy goodness and loving-kindness to us, and to all men. We bless Thee for our creation, preservation, and all the blessings of this life ; but above all, for Thine inestimable love in the redemption of the world by our Lord Jesus Christ ; for the means of grace, and for the hope of glory. And, we beseech Thee, give us that due sense of all Thy mercies, that our hearts may be unfeignedly thankful, and that we shew forth Thy praise, not only with our lips, but in our lives ; by giving up ourselves to Thy service, and by walking before Thee in holiness and righteousness all our days, through Jesus Christ our Lord, to Whom, with Thee and the Holy Ghost, be all honour and glory, world without end.   *Amen.*

> My God, I thank Thee, who hast made
>   The earth so bright ;
> So full of splendour and of joy,
>   Beauty and light,
> So many glorious things are here,
>   Noble and right.
>
> I thank Thee, too, that Thou hast made
>   Joy to abound ;
> So many gentle thoughts and deeds
>   Circling us round,
> That in the darkest spot of earth
>   Some love is found.
>
> I thank Thee more that all our joy
>   Is touch'd with pain ;
> That shadows fell on brightest hours ;
>   That thorns remain ;
> So that earth's bliss may be our guide,
>   And not our chain.

Suggestive Outlines. 151

THANKSGIVING.

"SEVEN times a day do I praise Thee."—*Psa.* cxix. 164.

READ—Exod. xv. 1-21.
 1 Chron. xxix. 10-18.
 Psa. cxii., cxiii.
 Rev. vii. 9-13.

Prayer.

IT is very meet, right, and our bounden duty, that we should at all times, and in all places, give thanks unto Thee, O Lord, Holy Father, Almighty, Everlasting God. Therefore, with Angels and Archangels, and with all the company of Heaven, we laud and magnify Thy glorious name; evermore praising Thee, and saying, Holy, holy, holy, Lord God of hosts, heaven and earth are full of Thy glory: glory be to Thee, O Lord most high. *Amen.*

PRAISE, my soul, the King of heaven;
 To His feet thy tribute bring,
Ransom'd, heal'd, restored, forgiven,
 Who like thee His praise shall sing?
  Praise Him, praise Him,
  Praise the everlasting King.

Praise Him for His grace and favour
 To our fathers in distress;
Praise Him still the same as ever,
 Slow to chide, and swift to bless;
  Praise Him, praise Him,
  Glorious in His faithfulness.

Father-like He tends and spares us;
 Well our feeble frame He knows;
In His hands He gently bears us,
 Rescues us from all our foes:
  Praise Him, praise Him,
  Widely as His mercy flow

Books Lately Published.

Second Edition, crown 8vo, 2s. 6d. extra cloth.

Footprints of the Saviour.

BY THE
REV. W. BOYD CARPENTER, M.A.,
Vicar of St. James's, Holloway.

CONTENTS:

1. BETHLEHEM.
2. CANA.
3. SYCHAR.
4. NAZARETH.
5. CAPERNAUM.
6. GENNESARET.
7. DECAPOLIS.
8. BETHANY.
9. GETHSEMANE.
10. CALVARY.
11. EMMAUS.
12. OLIVET.

With Thirteen Page Illustrations,

INCLUDING

The Walk to Emmaus,

BY GUSTAVE DORE.

Copied by permission of Messrs. Cassell, Petter, & Galpin.

The Rev. C. H. Spurgeon, in the *Sword and Trowel,* says: "In this attractive volume we commence at Bethlehem, Cana, and other sacred spots, and close at Emmaus and Olivet. . . . Full of a mild, quiet poetry of holy thought; not the torrent of Kishon, but the waters of Siloah, which go softly. Very many will be instructed, comforted, and encouraged by these holy words."

HAMILTON, ADAMS, & CO., 32, PATERNOSTER ROW.

Works by the Rev. Daniel March, D.D.

Third Edition, Crown 8vo., with Illustrations, 3s. 6d. cloth.

NIGHT UNTO NIGHT:

A Selection of Bible Scenes.

By REV. DANIEL MARCH, D.D.

Part I.—1. The Teachings of Night. 2. The Last Night of Sodom. 3. Abraham's Night Vision at Beersheba. 4. Jacob's Night at Bethel. 5. Jacob's Night of Wrestling. 6. The Last Night of Israel in Egypt. 7. The Night Passage of the Sea. 8. Saul's Night at Endor. 9. David's Night at the Jordan. 10. Elijah's Night in the Desert. 11. Jonah's Night at Nineveh. 12. The Night Watch on Mount Seir. 13. The Night of Tears. 14. The Night Feast of Belshazzar.

Part II.—1. A Night with Jesus at Jerusalem. 2. A Night of Prayer on the Mountain. 3. Night Storm on the Sea. 4. The Night of Peter's Temptation. 5. The Night of Agony in Gethsemane. 6. The First Night after the Resurrection. 7. The Night of Fruitless Toil. 8. Angel Visits in the Night. 9. Midnight in the Prison at Philippi. 10. Paul's Night on the Deep. 11. No Night in Heaven.

"Certain well-known Night Scenes of Scripture are here sketched with a vividness and graphic force which make us spectators of the varied incidents; while the lessons that are drawn from them of warning, of hope, or of duty, are brought home to the heart and conscience with tenderness and power."
British Quarterly Review.

"Dr. March has vividly conceived, and very graphically described, many Bible Scenes which were associated with the night, both in the Old and New Testaments. The fact of Dr. March's personal visit to the lands of the Bible enables him to speak with authority upon many matters. The whole book is suggestive and striking."
Literary World.

"The Nights of the Bible have a strange amount of doing and suffering connected with them, and it is to the lessons which are to be drawn from these wonderful pieces of night-work that Dr. March has sought to turn the reader's attention."
The Rock.

London: HAMILTON, ADAMS, & Co., 32, Paternoster Row.

Works by the Rev. Daniel March, D.D.

Fourth Edition, with Illustrations, Crown 8vo., 2s. 6d. cloth.

Walks and Homes of Jesus.

By Rev. DANIEL MARCH, D.D.

A few copies on toned paper, extra cloth, gilt edges, 3s. 6d.

"I regard the 'Walks and Homes of Jesus' as a very interesting and valuable work. The plan is new; the style is very attractive; the reflections are very just; and the whole character of the work such as is fitted to make a good impression. . . . Dr. March is an eloquent preacher, a fine scholar, and a most excellent man." ALBERT BARNES.

"Taking the Gospel record for his guide, and keeping the present aspect of Palestine ever in mind, Dr. March introduces us to Bethlehem, Nazareth, Capernaum, Bethesda, Tabor, Jericho, Bethany, and Jerusalem, and traces the walks of Jesus with men. . . . The descriptive passages are not fancy sketches. The fine imagination of the writer has indeed given life and reality to his descriptions, but truth has not been sacrificed to pictorial effect. The plan on which the book has been formed is, to us, original: the conception good, and the style reminds us of the late Dr. Hamilton." *Christian World.*

"Dr. March's object, in the 'Walks and Homes of Jesus,' has been to look upon our Lord as He was seen by the men of His time, and to combine with this view the more mature and instructed impressions which spring from faith in His redeeming work and His Divine nature. He is obviously very familiar with the physical aspect of Palestine, and describes, often in a very graphic manner, the different places where our Lord sojourned. . . . Altogether, it is a popular and highly readable presentation of the life of Him to whom we owe every blessing, and whose glory, when seen with the spiritual eye, fills the heart with wonder and the lips with praise."
Reformed Presbyterian Review.

"Step by step we are conducted through the vale of humiliation, from Bethlehem to Jerusalem—from the manger to the cross. Our interest is not allowed to flag throughout the journey, and often our hearts are made to burn within us as we walk with Jesus in the way." *Weekly Review.*

"Teems with the deepest devotional thought, called up by the contemplation of the scenes of our blessed Lord's ministry."
The Rock.

London: HAMILTON, & ADAMS, Co., 32, Paternoster Row.

Works by the late Albert Barnes.

THE LATE ALBERT BARNES' LAST WORK.

(Copyright in Great Britain, Ireland, and the Colonies.)

In Crown 8vo., with 24 Engravings, 508 pages, 5s. cloth.

SCENES AND INCIDENTS

IN THE

LIFE OF SAINT PAUL,

By ALBERT BARNES.

With a New Steel Portrait of the Author,

Which Mr. Barnes, writing under date August 12th, 1869, says, "*is decidedly the best likeness*, in my judgment and in that of my family, that has ever been taken of me."

> I. Early training of the Apostle Paul.—II. Saul a Persecutor. — III. His Conversion. — IV. Obedience to the Heavenly Vision.—V. Residence in Arabia.—VI. Saul brought to Antioch.—VII. Saul and Barnabas sent forth—VIII.—Paul and Silas at Philippi.—IX. Paul at Athens.—X. Paul at Corinth.—XI. Paul at Ephesus.—XII. Paul at Miletus.—XIII. Paul in the Temple at Jerusalem.—XIV. Paul before the Sanhedrim.—XV. Paul in the Castle at Jerusalem.—XVI. Paul before Felix.—XVII. Paul before Festus.—XVIII. Paul before Agrippa.—XIX. The Voyage to Rome.—XX. Paul at Malta.—XXI.—Paul in Rome.—XXII. First Trial before Nero.—XXIII. Paul's Anticipation of Death.—XXIV. Death of the Apostle Paul.

"Mr. Albert Barnes's style of writing in Notes and Commentaries, homilies and sermons, is too well known to need special description. He now offers us in a well-printed, goodly volume of nearly five hundred pages, a life of the famous Apostle of the Gentiles. The story of that wondrous life is here related for us rather diffusely, but carefully, and at times with some considerable freshness and power. Mr. Barnes has clearly consulted all the best authorities on his most important and interesting subject, and mingled with the facts of biography a view of original and devout reflection which accords well with the biography."—*Standard*.

London: HAMILTON, ADAMS, & Co., 32, Paternoster Row.

Works by the late Albert Barnes.

New Edition, Crown 8vo, 474 pp., 3s. 6d. cloth.

THE WAY OF SALVATION,
Illustrated and Explained.

"I commit this volume to the public with the hope that it may be found to be a safe guide on the most momentous inquiry which can come before the human mind. I have abundant occasion for gratitude for the manner in which the volumes that I have published heretofore have been received by the British public, as well as by my own countrymen; and I would hope that this volume may contribute something to the diffusion of the knowledge of the great principles of religious duty and doctrine which it has been the labour of my life to illustrate and defend." ALBERT BARNES.

Essays on Science and Theology.

Crown 8vo, 376 pp., 3s. 6d. cloth.

"The Author has given his cordial sanction to the publishing of this Edition, and has expressed his approbation of the selection and general arrangement of the Essays in their present form. In preparing them for the English public, I have considered it advisable to transpose them, as it appeared that, by an alteration in their sequence, a unity of design might be preserved which would render the work more attractive and profitable as a whole. By such arrangement, the Author's views are first given as to the historic progress and actual condition of literature and science, particularly in his own country, as well as the bearing which these have upon the interests of religion. After these general remarks, the reader's attention is called to the Desire of Reputation, which is so powerful a motive and so active an auxiliary to the pursuit of knowledge. The Choice of a Profession naturally presents itself as the next theme of consideration; and this Essay I would especially recommend for the forcible and practical remarks which are embodied in it. For such as have chosen the ministerial profession, the next section will have peculiar interest. The four following Essays are replete with most valuable remarks on various theological points connected with the defence and integrity of the faith; and those at the conclusion are mainly designed to set forth the kind of preaching which is most needed to meet the wants of the present age, and to subserve the great end of the gospel-ministry in the winning of immortal souls."—*Editor's Preface.*

London: HAMILTON, ADAMS, & Co., 32, Paternoster Row.

Works lately Published.

Dedicated by permission to the Archbishop of Canterbury.

Fourth Edition, Crown 8vo., toned paper, 2s. 6d. cloth.

AGNES AND THE LITTLE KEY

OR,

Bereaved Parents Instructed and Comforted.

WITH A RECOMMENDATORY PREFACE

By MISS MARSH.

" It is the tone of simple truth, the *reality* in this record of an earthly sorrow, gradually gilded and finally glorified by a Heavenly Hope and Faith, which renders it peculiarly suitable to mourners. Just enough of the anguish of a wounded heart is expressed to prove that no mere passing pang was inflicted by the loss of the 'desire' of those parents' eyes.' And in their efforts 'to comfort them which were in any trouble by the comfort wherewith they themselves were comforted of God,' there is none of that didactic strain of dry, theological consolation, or hard, unsympathising denunciation of all impassioned grief—too frequently the tone assumed in books written for mourners—which has made many a stricken soul exclaim, 'Thou speakest as one who has never lost a son.' "—*Miss Marsh's Preface.*

" We can well understand how this touching story, unfolded in these pathetic pages, has become so popular as to ask for itself a fourth edition, which it has now reached. The few incidents recorded, and the beauty of holiness which graces and glorifies the whole tissue of the story, cannot fail to make pleasant and useful impressions on the reader. The passages of poetry, and of Scripture, introduced for illustrative purposes, are extremely well chosen, and very apt for the purpose."
Rock.

" It is a sweet and holy-hearted book. Its first pages seemed to us over sentimental, perhaps trivial,—but *we*, thank God, have never tasted the bitterness this father has known, and we were not in prepared sympathy with the writer. On reading further, our feelings quite changed; and we now speak of it with tenderness and admiration."—*Nonconformist.*

London: HAMILTON, ADAMS, & CO., 32, Paternoster Row.

Works lately Published.

The Author's Dedication.

"To the Younger Members of my Congregation (friends and acquaintances of Catharine), and to every Father having a Daughter in Heaven, these pages are affectionately inscribed."

In Crown 8vo., printed on toned paper, 2s. 6d. extra cloth, uniform with "Agnes and the Little Key."

CATHARINE;
OR,
More than Conqueror.

By the Author of
"AGNES AND THE LITTLE KEY."

" Dear, beauteous Death, the jewel of the just,
   Shining nowhere but in the dark,
What mysteries do lie beyond thy dust,
   Could men outlook that mark!
He that hath found some fledged bird's-nest, may know,
   At first sight, if the bird be flown;
But what fair field, or grove, he sings in now,
   That is to him unknown."

Outline of Contents:—(1) More than Conqueror. (2) The Fear of Death alleviated. (3) The Search for the Departed. (4) The Silence of the Dead. (5) The Redemption of the Body.

"Those who have read '*Agnes and the Little Key*' will need no introduction to the ensuing pages. . . It is true, they will miss, as the author has done, the tender and judicious companion who mourned over her infant's grave, but who helped him to rejoice with Christian hope, and to tread in the path of Christian effort. Yet they will see that the same consolations could be experienced, when she was no longer at his side to partake and to promote them. The soul, which is sustained by a heavenly Comforter, is never alone in its sorrow.

" In the present work there will be found less of incident and action, but not less of true sympathy and of wisely-suggested counsel for the mourner. It contains ideas which all may read with interest, and all ponder with advantage."

London: HAMILTON, ADAMS, & Co., 32, Paternoster Row.

Works lately Published.

In large type, Crown 8vo., 1s. 6d. cloth.

SUNSET THOUGHTS;
OR,
Bible Narratives for the Aged.

1. ISAAC; or, Eventide.—2. LOT; or Harvest-time.—3. METHUSELAH; or, Length of Days.—4. ELIZABETH; or, Holiness of Life.—5. DAVID; or, Old and Grey-headed. 6. DEBORAH; or, Old and Faithful.—7. CALEB; or, Aged and Vigorous.—8. BARZILLAI; or Aged and Infirm.—9. JACOB; or, An Old Man's Memories.—10. PAUL; or, An Old Man's Hope.—11. ELI; or, Old Age Sorrowing.—12. SAMUEL; or, Old Age Honoured.—13. ESTHER; or, Danger and Deliverance.—14. HANNAH; or, Prayer and Praise.—15. JOB; or, Life's Changes.—16. ABRAHAM; or, Life's Trials.—17. ASA; or, the Sick Bed.—18. JOHN; or, the Beloved Disciple.—19. LEMUEL'S MOTHER; or, A Queen's Advice.—20. LAPIDOTH'S WIFE; or, A Mother in Israel.—21. MATTHEW; or, The Saviour's Call.—22. PETER; or, Growth in Grace.—23. ANNA; or, Life's Waiting-time.—24. MOSES; or, Canaan in Sight.

"The type is large and clear, to avoid fatiguing the eyes of the class of readers for whom this work is specially intended. It would prove an excellent present for a Christian advanced in years. We selected one of that description to give an opinion of it, and in return had it spoken of in terms of unqualified commendation."—*Weekly Review.*

2s. cloth; 3s. 6d. morocco (390 pages, 16mo.).

DAILY BIBLE TEACHINGS.
By T. S. HENDERSON.

"I have looked over the book carefully, and I have no hesitation in speaking of it as the best of its kind I have ever seen. The language is simple and forcible, the illustrations apt. The book is invaluable for use in schools and families." HENRY LEWIS, *Training College, Battersea.*

London: HAMILTON, ADAMS, & Co., 32, Paternoster Row.

www.ingramcontent.com/pod-product-compliance
Lightning Source LLC
Chambersburg PA
CBHW030435190426
43202CB00036B/886